The Biology of
Human Freedom

*Understanding the Genetic Foundations of
Self-Ownership*

Hugh A. Thomas

Glacier Publishing
P.O. Box 17512
Missoula, Montana 59808

ISBN: 0692205667
ISBN 13: 9780692205662
Library of Congress Control Number: 2014904857
Glacier Publishing, Stevensville, MT

Table of Contents

Introduction

In your childhood you were shown a portrait of yourself. This portrait was most likely a fuzzy image without detail, like a painting behind an oily and greasy pane of glass. There was a light emanating from your portrait, but the details were too obscure for you to gain any understanding.

As you got older, you discovered that your portrait was not behind a single pane of glass, but behind several panes. You made several attempts to clean the first pane only to find another layer of smudged glass, making your vision of yourself forever obscure. The more you cleaned, that is, the more you tried to understand, the more out-of-focus your portrait became. All attempts to clean the glass panes were futile; you never developed a clear picture of your real nature.

Now imagine, and only for a brief moment, that you can clearly see the *real you*. You will see an image of a being of great intelligence, a being that commands the most powerful mind of all life forms, and a being that is capable of the highest feats of mental powers of any species of life in the known universe. This being is capable of a great amount of love and understanding, a great amount of charity and thoughtfulness, both for itself, and for all living things. This being has no inherited guilt and no envy, and this being is unique, in that, *there will never be another.*

This book is intended to be a guide that will give you the tools needed to clean your portrait so that you can achieve a clearer vision of who you really are. Consider every chapter a mental device that will help clean another layer so that your vision of yourself becomes more defined. After a time, you will have removed some of this oil and grease. Hopefully, you will then realize that the veil that covers your self-image is actually a complex fabric woven from delusions and lies, and that this fabric has been blocking your vision of your true nature. You might also see that these delusions and lies are created by the misanthropists of the world, that is, by those humans who hate their own species. You will learn that these misanthropists are pathogens to your biology; that they can degrade your energy, twist your mind, and that they oftentimes kill.

This book will give you the conceptual *tools* needed to clean your portrait, however, the mental *work* of understanding is your responsibility. This book is not complete. Human nature is far too complex to explain in one book or a hundred books.

It is my hope that, in these pages, and by your mental work, you can see a road that leads you to a better understanding of your powers. If you agree and decide to take this road, you might find that, in the future, you will make new roads yourself.

———

Read history and you will be reading mostly the history of regimes and the misery they generate. Usually, there is a period of relative peace, and then murder within the regime (purging) or murder between regimes (war) ensues, with more murders after the victors take control and the cleansing begins.

Governments murder far more of their own citizens internally than they kill by war. Using rough and generally accepted numbers, a total of about 130 million people were killed in World War I, World War II, the Vietnam War, the Soviet War in Afghanistan, the Korean War, and a few others.

Compare this to over 200 million people killed by internal, politically motivated murders in the same time period. This includes the brutal regimes of Mao, Stalin, Hitler and Pol Pot. There are many more.

Surely, the deaths by governments of over 300 million people in the last 100 years would be worthwhile teaching in public schools. However, little of this is taught. It is not difficult to understand the reasoning: Public schools are government schools and governments strive to obscure their own predispositions.

Internal murders, that is, political murders, are nothing more than an attempt to change human nature or perceived bad thinking. Some people just will not accept the philosophy of the regime. They must be eliminated. Many times, whole ethnic groups will be exterminated because of the belief that they are inferior. This inferiority is nearly always a perceived inferiority in thinking. They will have the wrong religion, or are a member of the wrong class. This extermination of wrong-thinking people partially forms the foundation for the motives of all mass murderers.

However, all dictatorships have an even deeper underlying motive. This motive is the desire to obliterate the attributes of human nature that involve self-ownership.

Humans have the genetic propensity for self-ownership and the ownership of property. These traits are the antithesis of those who wish to achieve ultimate power. This hunger for power is usually hidden by claims of higher motives, such as income equality, race superiority, collectivism, nationalism, environmentalism and more.

Currently, Americans are faced with the threat of a fascist form of socialism. The goal of state control of all humans is cloaked in the ideas of equality of income, medical care for all and protection of the environment. The "greedy business class" must be controlled, poverty must be erased, and the state must provide all medical care. The outcome will, based on history, be murder and poverty on a vast scale.

———

Animals have a sense of self-ownership in that they will battle to protect the self, that is, their own lives. This sense of self in the human animal is in conflict with the state's goals. Hence, the state usually disarms the citizens prior to the purging of those who resist the state's authority. Much of this disarming begins with intellectual disarming via the public schools.

We can arbitrarily divide individuals into two groups: the populace that seeks to practice their self-ownership and the politicians and their minions who seek to conquer this aspect of human nature. They see self-ownership, that is, self-rule, as the prize to be controlled and destroyed. Their depravity is rarely understood until it is too late.

This depravity likely stems from their lack of a sense of efficacy towards reality. They are poor at rebuilding a carburetor, repairing a roof, tilling a field, conducting scientific research, or working in a factory. In these skills they are incompetent or uncomfortable. What they do have is a great ability for deception and a deep feeling that is the hatred and resentment of those who are competent. They were most likely manipulative as children, and as this manipulative behavior is honed in their young years, they may later take up positions as corporate leaders, bureaucrats or politicians. Because they feel inept with the normal tasks of life, they turn to the control of those who are more practical. In the most extreme cases, their hatred compels them to destroy. This intense compulsion drives them to the top of the heap. These are the perverts of the human race. Their perversion has a name, *misanthropy*, the hatred of human beings.

Your natural tendency is to remain autonomous and protect your life. This natural independence, the sovereignty that is programmed into your biology, is rapidly becoming the target of an over reaching government.

———

My goal is to keep this book as simple as possible while at the same time giving the reader a full understanding of their self-ownership. There is a demonstrable basis for self-ownership, and this is a testable fact throughout nature.

Best wishes,
Hugh A. Thomas
January 2014

1
You

You are a living biological organism. Every atom in your body, with the exception of the non-human matter, that is, the dust in your hair, the tag-along microbes, and the dirt under your fingernails, has biological associations.

Your DNA is a molecule that encodes the genetic instructions used in the development and functioning of all your body's processes. All life has, at its core, a specific DNA molecule that instructs cells how to develop and how to function. DNA is the blueprint, the program, the road map for your body's physical life. Your DNA is much like the DNA of other living species. Your DNA is identical to 98% of the DNA of a chimpanzee,[1] 90% of your housecat and 60% of a banana plant.[2] This is not that striking when you consider that a chimp needs to collect and digest food, have sex and offspring, see and feel, and make judgments about distance, weather, and much more. A banana plant also makes offspring, and makes judgments about weather, soil moisture, direction of the sun, etc. That you share much of your DNA with other species is not accidental. All species of life have similar goals.

For hundreds of millions of years, plants and animals have developed self-defense skills. Many species of plants and animals have also developed a sense of private property and skills for the defense of this property. This is fundamental. Humans, like many other animals and plants, have a natural propensity to defend property. As strange as it might seem, and as you will see later, many species of plants defend their area (real estate) against invaders. Defense of self and property is a function of many plants and animals, and these functions are hard-wired into their DNA.

That humans will fight to retain their property and lives, that even a small child will react with panic when a toy is taken from him, shows that humans must be genetically wired for the defense of self and the possession of property. The evidence is in thousands of species that share human DNA. That the specific genes haven't been isolated is not a concern, as the anecdotal and circumstantial evidence is overwhelming. These genetic controls that guide the self-directing and self-preserving actions that plants, animals and humans display are the recipe for the concept we call "self-ownership."

For thousands of years, humans have been at war with a few errant individuals who have attempted to subvert human nature by erasing this genetic tendency towards self-ownership. This war is a war against your biology, against your life. This epic battle is a fight between your nature and the desires of a few depraved individuals and their many delusional followers who want to stuff you into a mold created by their delusional thinking, a mold that requires your enslavement and a mold that is contrary to your nature. This mold has many names: socialism, communism, fascism, imperialism, nationalism, monarchy, etc. Regardless of the name used, the goal is always the same: the erasure of self-ownership.

———

Only the individual brain has understanding. Therefore, this book is about you, the reader, an individual human being.

There is no collective thinking or knowledge. If a group of 20 people are asked to add two numbers, there will be 20 individual brains all thinking independently of each other, with each brain making its own calculations.

Human brains do not work together; they are separated by physical space. Ask any neurologist or read a textbook on brain science: There is no evidence of minds or brains converging to create a collective consciousness. *Your brain's processes are separate from other people's brain processes.* To say otherwise is only a vacant claim with no supporting evidence.

If one were to make the extraordinary claim that there are herds of pink unicorns on Mars, you would ask for evidence. Why not do the same for the extraordinary claim that there is a "collective mind?"

Your brain is alone and not networked with other brains. Your brain chemistry, the neurons, synapses and electrical currents are independent of other people's brain processes. These processes are isolated and contained by the bone that is your skull. There is no evidence that your brain's neurons, chemistry and electrical currents can penetrate this bone barrier, magically travel around in space, penetrate other people's skulls, and integrate with their brain chemistry and neurons and become meaningful knowledge. There is no collective brain function. Therefore, this book is directed at you, and you alone.

Some animals such as bees and ants do seem to have a collective structure. This phenomenon has been documented by science. These insects communicate by body movements, pheromones and other physical and chemical signals to achieve one goal. However, you are a human and not an insect. To claim that humans ought to function collectively like a beehive is just as irrational as supposing all humans must take to the air and pollinate flowers.

For the nitpickers among us, one could say that there are chemical signals passed from one human to another. For example, some human pheromones are thought to play a role in sexual signaling. Notice however, that these signals are outside the brain, they are not knowledge, and are fundamentally no different than a signal sent by a urinating dog to mark territory.

Before you can understand why freedom is mandated by your nature, you must first understand a few things about yourself. You will never be successful in musing about these things if you have incorrect ideas regarding your nature and the nature of human beings in general.

Only individuals exist in the real world, and you are one of them. This concept we hold in our minds, the concept "society" is a mental vapor, a mental construct. Society is a word that exists inside your mind, and is created by your thoughts. Individual human beings exist *outside* your mind. You and other individuals are real, "society" is a mental abstraction that is only useful in discussion. This is easy. Think about it.

Since there is no such thing as a collective human brain, since you are not a termite or bee, then we must look at you, the individual human, and ask questions that concern your basic nature and then offer understandable answers.

You are a living organism, a biological organism. This makes you unique in that, on planet Earth, living organisms comprise a minute percentage of the total mass of the planet, and, as far as it is known, a minuscule amount of the universe as a whole. You are also unique in that your brain has the greatest computing power of all known organisms. There are well over fifteen million species of life on Earth and you stand above all the rest with your mental powers. It has been estimated that the human brain can make 20 million billion computations per second.[3,4] This is a gigantic achievement. You ought to be very proud to be a human.

However, you are fragile. Just falling a few feet can mean death. Going without water for a few days can mean death, and being in the wrong place can be fatal. Your life is precarious and fleeting; your life duration is only a flicker in time compared to the age of the Earth and the universe.

You are a living organism that faces conscious choices every day. A bacterium does not face these conscious choices. Only higher animals have conscious choices they must make.

Most animals have strong instincts that guide them along in their decisions. Humans have little if any instincts, and as far as it is known, humans are born basically *"tabula rasa,"* that is, with a blank slate. Based on this model, you have no automated knowledge, and you need and ought to find the best knowledge available in order to have a successful life. More knowledge results in fewer mistakes.

All of your attributes are biological attributes. There is nothing about your life that is not biological. All of your property has a biological function. Your clothes have a biological function in that they protect your body. Your car and bicycle have biological functions that replace the efforts of walking. Your house has a biological function in that it is a shelter for your life.

If some thought is applied to this idea, the idea that you are a living biological organism and everything significant in your life has a biological function, it becomes evident that biology is what you ought to be concerned about.

To live a life of understanding, you need to be a biologist of the most basic kind. You need to ask and find answers to many questions about how the rest of nature affects your biology. You need to understand the biological functions of production, the storage of your production, its trade, and politics. You need to understand that money, for example, is actually an attribute of your biology.

You face a hostile nature every day. You face hostile people and hostile governments. You also face your own ignorance of these things, an ignorance that is not a moral fault of your own, but rather an ignorance that is the lack of knowledge. Much of the knowledge you need has never been defined or has been denied to you by public schools and by parents who suffer the same problems as you do. Bad philosophy and ignorance are carried forth from generation to generation. This fact requires no proof other than the observation that war, suffering and murder has dominated all of human history.

Because you are born with little or no instincts that tell you how to live, you need to take the effort to learn some of these basic facts. This learning is a neurological process. Remember, your neurological functions are isolated from others, so it is your responsibility to do the conceptual work yourself. Building your knowledge takes effort. It is work, and not always enjoyable. You will need to turn off your television, put away your game controller, get off the internet and think on your own. No one else can do this for you.

Your brain is a collection of atoms. These atoms are arranged in ways that can be described by physical law and are the building blocks of the molecules that make up your brain's cells. These cells create chemicals and generate electrical currents that control your thinking and bodily functions. When you think about how your mind works, stop for a moment and realize that these trillions of atoms have merged together in such a complex way that they can actually think about themselves. This fact alone is possibly the most amazing feature of human existence.

You are a sack of chemical compounds that is self-propelled and self-conscious. You are made of atoms, and these atoms have formed into a biological organism that is self-aware. This is who you are; it is *everything* you are, *there is nothing else*, and you have no measurable or testable evidence to the contrary.

You have a psychology. This psychology is an attribute of higher animals. Monkeys, dogs, cats and many other animals have a psychology. If you own a cat or a dog, you know this is true. They are not machines; they have feelings. These feelings are what make life worth living. They give us the joy and desire to keep going. You seek pleasure, you want to be free, and freedom is the greatest pleasure.

Notice that these feelings can also send warning signals. The brain is capable of an incredible amount of calculations of which we are not fully aware. Sometimes these warning signals are just a feeling of uneasiness. Have you had any of these feelings recently?

All biological organisms have challenges. Your challenge is to gain the knowledge about your biology and how it relates to other people, how it relates to the economy, to the government, and freedom.

The magnificent powerhouse that is your brain gives you the ability to prolifically create. The millions of other species of life on Earth pale in comparison. It has been shown that a few higher animals can think in creative ways. However, the human mind can instantly make random connections of dissimilar ideas and merge these into new discoveries and new ways of doing things. Tools are invented, music is created and new medicines abound.

With the exception of humans, animals have a tightly controlled way of perceiving the world and a tightly controlled way of acting on physical reality. Much of their thinking is automatic. A bear will instinctively eat in excess of his current needs in order to gain body fat to survive the coming winter. Humans must think this process through and make a conscious decision to store food for the future. With this in mind, it is easy to see that humans are much freer thinkers than other animals. Animals rely on instinct for much of their decision-making, whereas humans must make a conscious decision to engage their minds. This conceptual work is not fully automatic. Mistakes can and will be made.

When an animal makes a mistake due to faulty instincts, instincts that are not in line with physical reality, the outcome is often the elimination of that animal and the offspring that might carry this defect. A poor decision by a human can carry misfortune as well, even illness or death. If these faulty decisions and incorrect concepts are accepted by a large group of people, the illnesses are suffered by all.

This faulty thinking arises when you permit this high-powered human creativity to turn inward toward concepts that involve feelings, emotions, vague thoughts and unproven assumptions. In spending excessive time attempting to make sense of these vague thoughts that do not involve referents to external reality, you can create a delusional realm. This mode of thinking has been a plague on humans as the historical record shows. Conversely, when you turn your thinking outward toward physical reality, you gain a firmer grasp of the truth.

People tend to believe things they hear over and over again, even if these things are irrational. Children are very susceptible to this problem. Demonology, witchcraft, spell casting, original sin, conjuring the dead, black magic, religion — all of these things and many more are held by the great majority of individuals. If you believe in any idea that has no connection to physical reality, you ought to reexamine your assumptions. For example, if someone claims your neighbor is a witch, reject the idea until you have a physical proof that can be tested by experiment and repeated by another independent experimenter. First, you know your neighbor is made of atoms. How are these atoms arranged differently in your neighbor than in yourself? She must have some form of energy source that differs from yours. What is this energy? Is it electrical? Do you have the measurements? Can these measurements be used in an experiment?

Much of human misery is based on beliefs that are accepted by the masses without proof.

All of us will get sick, grow old and die. Cancer, tuberculosis, heart disease, a multitude of infectious agents or old age will kill us all. If we disregard these diseases and old age, what remains is death by delusional thinking. This delusional thinking is the weapon used by the humans who prey on their own species. Their goal is to convince you of some delusion. All dictatorships and the murder they bring —murders by war or murders of their own subjects — are based on delusion. Hitler's delusional thinking involved the pushing of the irrational belief that Jews were inferior and the Arian race was superior. There was no testable evidence for this belief. As a result, fifty million died in World War II. Karl Marx had no testable evidence of the existence of "the collective," but 200 million people were slaughtered by communist zealots.

There is no evidence that humans are unnatural to Earth, but many of the environmentalists wish to depopulate the Earth. *Depopulate* is another word for *elimination*.

At this time, little is known concerning the actual physical processes undertaken by the brain in complex thought. Considering the complexity involved, neurology, in its current state, is a very crude science. Mr. Jones may arrive at a correct conclusion to a problem by using a different set of brain cells than Mr. Smith. Billions of neurons will be involved. What all of these neurons are doing is beyond current science. What can be offered are examples of thought that *do not* contradict the evidence, and then examples that *do* contradict the evidence. With this held in mind, one can then come to reasonable conclusions about a few valid ways of thinking.

2
You Against Yourself — Your Greatest Delusions

Man is the delusional animal.

It has been said many times that *man is the rational animal*. This is true in part, but might porpoises and chimpanzees also be rational? We really don't know for sure at this time because we cannot know exactly what is going on inside their brains. However, we do know for a fact that porpoises, chimpanzees and many other animals can solve problems, and this implies that they do employ reason, that they are rational.

The possibility that animals can be delusional is much more difficult to evaluate. We do not know if a chimpanzee, porpoise or a fish have delusions. We know animals can make mistakes, but these mistakes are not necessarily delusions. However, we do know that man is delusional, and this can be proven. Consequently, the definition of man as being the *delusional animal* is more reasonable.

When faced with a highly complex existence, and when answers to the complexity of the universe are unavailable, humans often turn to emotional intuition and delusional thinking is the likely outcome. These delusions oftentimes embed themselves in the population and become self-sustaining.

For example, until a few hundred years ago, it was believed that bloodletting was the best treatment for many diseases. Bloodletting was even practiced to treat loss of blood. What seems insane to us now was common practice for 2,000 years. It is easy to see that delusions can be dangerous. Delusions can be stubborn and can persist in your mind for years or a lifetime, and are most likely in the minds of everyone you know.

You need clear thinking

Before you can understand the nature of freedom you must correct any delusional thinking you might have concerning the nature of man. Progress is rejecting false ideas and building on that which is new and valid. You cannot understand your life and the idea of freedom if your knowledge base is built on delusions and contradictions. You need a knowledge base that is sound and consistent. You need a mental architecture that recognizes false assumptions and is willing to correct these false assumptions regardless of the emotional pain involved. You need the facts. You need the truth. Whatever this truth is, you need to be willing to let this truth be your guide.

Your thought experiment

Thought experiments have been used for centuries to tease out the truth in complex problems. For example, Albert Einstein used a thought experiment to discover his theory of relativity. Newton used thought experiments to arrive at his theory of gravity. Galileo and many others have shaped history by employing thought experiments in order to arrive at greater underlying truths.

Let us begin your first thought experiment by assuming there is a healthy newborn baby on a sandy beach. Assume this baby was just born to the last woman on Earth who happened to be the last human on Earth, and now this woman, the baby's mother, has been vaporized along with the rest of the human race. The baby is therefore the last human in existence. Further suppose a few space aliens from across the galaxy land on this beach. These aliens are the greatest scientific minds in the universe with a billion years of science behind them and they examine the baby. They scan every atom in the baby; they analyze every chemical and test every electrical current.

Now, a few questions:

1. Would the alien scientists find the "rights of man," "unalienable rights," or "individual rights" in the baby?
2. Would they find "original sin?"
3. Would they find that the baby has a "duty" or a "social contract?"
4. Would they find that the baby is unnatural to the planet Earth?
5. Would the scientists find something mysterious that is beyond the physical materials that make up the baby?

The answer to the above questions is "no." If you believe otherwise, then the burden is on you to demonstrate the existence of these attributes in the baby.

Just as in our example of pink unicorns on Mars, the burden of proof ought to be held by those who make any extraordinary claim.

For example, it is the government's burden to prove guilt in a criminal trial. It is the scientist's burden to prove any theory before it is considered valid. Einstein's theory of general relativity was considered oddball until validated by the measurable observations made in 1919 by Arthur Eddington. Until that time, many scientists were skeptical.

If you think the baby has rights as a part of its nature, then identify what gene in the baby's DNA contains these rights. If you believe these attributes are not in the baby's DNA, but reside elsewhere, then identify exactly where they are. You can't do so because these rights, and the imagined attributes of original sin, duty and unnaturalness, do not exist as part of the baby. These ideas exist only in your mind and they are called delusions.

Consider only the facts that our independent alien scientists would discover. Rights, original sin, unnaturalness and duty are not attributes of the baby and the scientists would not find them. These non-attributes are nothing more than delusions. Problems arise when these delusions are blindly swallowed by billions of humans and held for thousands of years. These delusions are the backbone of human misery and need to be eliminated from your thinking.

In our thought experiment, we isolated the baby, removed other humans and their subjective beliefs, brought in the best scientists in the universe that were not prone to fantasy, and then we imagined what the scientists concluded about the baby. We want the scientists to tell us what they find by objective measurement and verifiable evidence. We want reality. We do not want unfounded suspicion, witchcraft, voodoo, mysticism, irrational feelings or smoke and mirrors. We want the truth about the nature of the baby. *All of this truth is contained in the baby's biology.*

The baby is what he is and nothing more. This is important: The baby is made of atoms, his mind is receiving information about the external world via his senses, and this sensory data is processed by the innumerable cells, neurons, electrical currents, and chemistry in his brain. This is the evidence we have.

You cannot rationally claim there is more to the baby than what can be observed and/or inferred by what exists within the baby. If you believe there is "something more" that supersedes the baby's biology, for example, the "Spirit of Zoor," or "God's wishes for peace," a voodoo curse, original sin, or natural rights, then you have submitted to delusional thinking and the corresponding loss of freedom it always brings.

Freedom works only in an atmosphere of rational understanding. Freedom is not possible with everyone claiming the nature of man is whatever their feelings require at the moment.

Your greatest delusions — rights

In our above thought experiment it is easy to see that natural rights, unalienable rights or individual rights are not there. Rights are an emotional wish, a form of escapism that will put you in a state of denial. They are pure fantasy and dangerously delusional.

Let us use another thought experiment to demonstrate the power of emotion to create delusional thinking. As an aside experiment, answer the question following the thought experiment as quickly as possible — that is, give a "snap" answer.

The experiment: Assume the baby is alone on the beach and a man suddenly appears. He has a large club with spikes protruding from the end and he starts pounding on the baby's head. Answer quickly: Does the baby have the right to his own life?

This writer's quick answer is "yes," even though he knows better. It took many tries at this thought experiment to overcome the emotional wish for the baby to be safe. This is the power that emotion can bring to any situation involving our sense of empathy. We want the baby to be safe, we want the baby to be free of pain, we want him to have a good life. Because we care so much, our minds create rights for the baby, rights that are not there. Rights are an emotional wish. An emotional wish is not knowledge.

Consider the following emotional "rights" that are based on wishful thinking rather than reality:

1. Man has individual rights because he is a rational animal. He cannot be forced to think and needs reason in order to survive.
2. A redwood tree in an old growth forest has rights because it is old.
3. A person has the right to kill another if there is a suspicion of witchcraft.
4. A mother bird has the right to feed a baby bird.
5. One human has the right to love another.
6. The believer in one religion has the right to kill another person that believes in a different religion.
7. One race of people has the right to kill another race of people based on race supremacy.
8. A king has the divine right to enslave you because of his claims of royal blood or a direct connection with God.

It is very easy to see that having a strong emotion can trigger an emotional rights construct that is completely false. Well-meaning people, such as the Founding Fathers of the United States, create rights to life and property; the narcissists will create divine rights; the mystics will create religious rights and race rights; and the statists who want to destroy capitalism, as well as a large part of the human population, will create rights for animals, plants and the "environment."

Emotionally derived and irrationally created rights are the cause of much of the suffering in the human race. Hitler's claim that the Arian race had special rights to dominate others led to the deaths of fifty million people. The belief that the rights of "the environment" have precedence over humans, the belief that animals and plants have "rights" — these false claims to rights that don't exist have resulted and will result in epic historical disasters.

You have no natural rights, nor does any other person or group. If they claim to have rights over your life, regardless of their numbers, ten people or a million, the rights do not exist, and their claims are invalid.

These rights are delusional and have no connection to reality. Notice that your "natural right" to live as you please can interfere with a king's "divine right" to make you his slave. What happens when your "right to life" interferes with the "rights of the collective?" How do you prove these claimants are wrong and you are correct?

You can't. You can march on city hall, stomp your feet, become very emotional, or accuse everyone of being irrational and immoral; none of these things will change the facts.

You are your biology. If there are no rights in your biology, then you have no naturally occurring rights.

Intellectual honesty is accepting what is true. What is true is what exists.

Original sin

It is easy to see that our alien scientists would find no original sin in their investigations. If there is no original sin in the baby, then why do you hold to that idea so tightly? Why is there an underpinning of guilt that many humans feel?

Let's add to the thought experiment. Assume that the alien scientists arrive on the beach and find not only the baby, but also find a baby bird and a baby rabbit. Further assume that they perform an exhaustive investigation of these three animals. They look at every atom in each of the animals; they map the genomes. They examine the animals with the best scientific equipment in the universe.

Question: What would they find different in the human baby's structure that gives the human baby original sin, but not the bird? Would they find original sin in the rabbit?

Note that original sin means sin from the *origin,* that is, from birth. Now, what would be the motive for such a doctrine? If you wanted power over people, would it not be smart of tell them they are guilty because they were born and that they need *you* to save their souls?

If you swallow the doctrine of original sin, your psychology of life will be forever undermined. You will have no solid rock on which you can stand. If life is like crossing a fast moving stream, original sin will be the slimy bottom that forever diminishes your moral traction. You will feel guilt, and you will have a bias toward your fellow man. Original sin doctrine is an arbitrary and delusional construct designed to rob you of your self-worth and make you dependent on religion. After all, you need the church because you are defective from birth and need to be saved from your own evil nature. You are commanded to give the church your money and live your life in undeserved shame because of a delusional claim.

If religions were truthful, they would clearly spell out the facts on original sin. They would make it very clear, so clear that any eight-year-old child could understand it. However, even though original sin is the foundation of Christian doctrine, the idea is cloaked in obscurity and confusion. Ask any preacher or priest what original sin actually is, and they will be confused themselves. Demand they write it down. Demand they make it very clear why you must live your life with self-hatred and suspect everyone in your family and everyone in the human race. If you have a newborn baby, ask your minister why you ought to view this baby as defective.

Conviction in a court of law for petty theft or a traffic violation requires more evidence. There is no evidence for original sin, and yet millions believe humans are basically evil. They morally condemn all humans without objective, measureable evidence. It is no wonder war has dominated human history. Since they view human beings as basically evil, why not just kill a few million?

Original sin is not only a weight around your neck, but it also has huge political implications and makes possible much of the violence that has dominated human history, as we will see later.

Duty

Returning to the alien scientists in our thought experiment, imagine they arrive on Earth to find two newborn babies. The babies are minutes old and the last human beings on Earth. The scientists examine them extensively. Would they find that one baby has a duty to the other?

Further assume a newborn Reese's monkey appears, along with the two babies. Would the scientists find duty in the monkey? If you believe duty exists in the babies, but not in the monkey, what is different about the monkey that he has no duty, but the babies do? Consider that Reese's monkeys share about 99% of DNA with humans. What is different about the 1%?

If you still believe in rights, original sin and duty, I suggest you examine that 1% of human DNA and find those attributes in that DNA and report your findings to the world.

The Collective

If the aliens encountered two babies on the beach, would they detect a third entity known as "the collective?" Three babies? A million babies? If you believe they would, what sort of material is this collective made of? If it is not a solid material but some sort of energy or other force, what are the measurements? Did you have some sort of sensory input emanating from this collective, if so, what was this sensation? Did it come from one of your seven known senses?

The idea of the collective is a simple delusion. There is no evidence for it, it is only a term used by delusional minds. When a Leftist puts forth the idea of "the collective," many will accept the idea without any critical thought. They will just assume the validity of the idea. This simple delusion has resulted in horrific murders and suffering for millions.

Humans are unnatural

Suppose in their examination of the Earth, our alien scientists tested not only the baby, the rabbit and Reese's monkey, but also tested thousands of other animals and plants. Suppose they examined elephants, bears, tuna fish, birds and insects. Suppose that in all, they examined 50,000 different species.

Question: *What would they find in the baby's DNA, the baby's genome or anywhere in the baby's body that would make them believe all the 49,999 species they examined were natural to Earth, but the baby was "unnatural?"*

The answer is, of course, *nothing!* There is absolutely no evidence that humans and therefore human action is unnatural. Zero. No evidence whatsoever.

Notice the effect achieved when the delusion of original sin is combined with the delusion that holds the products of human action are not natural. In other words, you are evil at birth and what you create is not natural. Another way to say it would be: *You are not good and you are not natural, and you can never change.*

If evil exists, then surely, this is it. These delusional doctrines create a sense of disconnect to one's own life; they are alienating and are likely a prime source of great mental distress. No doubt, they have led to the failure of millions to achieve their full potential in life. *Any child that is taught these delusions is being abused.*

The major and defining attribute the alien scientists would discover within the human baby is a very large brain with a large capacity for critical thinking. They would also find this capacity and attribute in porpoises or dolphins. In fact, they might conclude that the human baby has the greatest mind of all animals on the land, and the porpoise the greatest mind of all the animals in the sea. Would they then conclude that the porpoise is "unnatural?"

If the alien scientists were to examine a beaver colony and discover that beavers cut down trees in order to build dams and lodges, would they conclude the beaver dam and lodge were "unnatural?" If not, then why do you think when a human cuts down trees in order to build a house that this structure is artificial? Why do you think the Hoover Dam is artificial and a beaver dam natural? The answer is: Because you are delusional!

Vague thoughts are valid evidence

You have the ability to introspect and think about *how* you are thinking. This introspection can take you into endless journeys of the mind. We can say that the mind is the thinking and conscious part of the brain.

The mind also includes our memories. You do not hold all of your memories in your consciousness, but only hold a few at the time, and many memories are buried and difficult to access.

It has been said that the human brain is the most complex machine known. Ben Carson, the well-known neurosurgeon, once said that a "mosquito's brain has a thousand times the computing power of a desktop computer."[5] Your brain is a million times larger than a mosquito's. Now, imagine the power of *your* brain.[6]

The mind is a feature of the brain, but the brain does much more than give us our mind. The brain is also involved with very complex actions to which you have no access. For example, your brain keeps you breathing while you sleep, but you can *will* yourself to stop breathing for a minute while you are awake. However, you have no access to that part of the brain that controls your hearing; you cannot will your brain to cancel your hearing.

Your brain is working without your permission twenty-four hours per day performing complex actions that keep you alive. Imagine the complexity of just taking a walk through the woods. Your brain must make a huge amount of calculations to just walk over uneven ground. Each of your eyes has over 100 million light-sensitive nerve cells in the retina, and these cells will be sending signals to your brain and your brain must quickly process and interpret these millions of signals to determine what is happening on the outside. Combine this with your inner ear's balancing function, where the brain must control balance and integrate this data with your vision and leg and arm muscles, and the complexity is enormous. This example is only a minuscule view of the brain's complexity.

The point is: You are only conscious of a very small portion of what your brain is doing.

Sometimes, the brain's enormous complexity will show itself. You have dreams, many of which make little sense, and you have feelings and emotions; oftentimes you may not know their origins. You might have a sense of déjà vu at times. Because of this complexity, it is easy to get a feeling that there is *something* deeper. After all, you might be aware of only one percent or less of your brain's activity, and this vague feeling is normal. However, vague feelings and a sense that *something else is there* are not proof of anything. For example, these vague feelings are what give you your nebulous sense that you have a soul. Would our alien scientists find a soul in the baby? If you think they would, would they also find a soul in a monkey? In a dog? In a fish? In a bacterium?

Your sense that there is *something else* is correct. However, your belief that this leakage of stray data into your mind has a "grand meaning" is delusional. Vague feelings do not equal soul, connection with the collective, mystic cosmos connections, voodoo or Mother Nature's vibes. It is this very leakage that lays the path for scam artists to trick you into their religions, cults and other phony endeavors.

Some results of human delusion

When environmentalists want to control everything you do, how you travel, what you eat and what you say, they cite animal *rights,* the *rights* of the environment, the *rights* of Mother Earth, and the claim that the products of human action are not *natural.*

When the Catholic Church sought to enslave and murder thousands in the Spanish Inquisition, the concept of *original sin* was motivating their actions.

For seventy-five years, the Left kept busy by mass murdering 200 million people while holding to the delusion that all people had a *duty* to the state and the communist *collective.*

The mental architecture that you must develop in order to think clearly is the same architecture used by scientists during the golden age of science. You need to understand that reality is determined by *what is there*, and only by, *what is there*.

If a rational doctor is confronted with an unknown disease, he looks for pathogens or abnormal cells, and he studies blood or heartbeat to determine what is wrong. He looks at physical reality to collect his evidence. Doctors in primitive societies that are entrenched with delusion might *assume* evil spirits, spells, etc., and correspondingly produce a treatment with disastrous results.

In New Guinea, there is a process of putting someone on trial where a possum is placed in a cage and offered a sweet potato. If the possum takes a bite of the sweet potato, then the person on trial is potentially guilty. Final guilt is determined by the cooking of caterpillars.[7] This is the danger of delusional thinking.

In a modern court of law ruled by reason, the attempt to introduce speculation about a possum eating a sweet potato during a trial would not be permitted and would be ruled "inadmissible." The New Guinea tribesmen are assuming the possum's appetite is linked to the guilt or innocence of a human. How could they assume such a crazy idea? Well, if you lived in a culture that believed vague thoughts determine the facts of reality, this dangerous and delusional thinking would be normal.

As in a court of law, *you must never assume facts that are not in evidence.* There is no evidence for natural rights. There is no evidence for duty. There is no evidence for you being unnatural to this Earth. There is no evidence for original sin, and there is no evidence for the existence of a collective.

———

A word about the above thought experiments. When we imagined the alien scientists with their high level of objectivity, and when we imagined that other humans and their delusions were not present, we were actually cleaning the rubbish out of our own minds so that we could see and think more clearly. We set our delusions and emotions aside and gave our rational minds free reign. Human delusion is so powerful that we need to get outside ourselves and pretend we are space aliens in order to think clearly!

If you cannot separate your delusions from the facts of reality, you will never be free psychologically, and you will never be a potent advocate of freedom for yourself and others.

3
You Against Nature

You can work against yourself by clinging to delusions, but you face another foe, the foe known as "nature." However, nature is not a good word for the overall problem you face; physical reality would be a better term.

You go to work, come home, watch television or read, check your computer for emails, have dinner and socialize with friends and family. You might go out to coach your daughter's basketball team or go to a bar a have some drinks. You are concerned with day-to-day things. You might spend a few moments thinking about your investments or human history, but your main concerns are family, home, work, friends, hobbies, etc. You are most likely focused on the short term and the events and conditions that affect you over a short time span.

You probably spend very little time thinking about your fragile existence. But realize this: *You are in danger at all times.*

There are some very thin and fragile wires bringing electric current to your house. These wires are a lifeline to you; they carry the energy that gives you light, the energy to keep your food from spoiling, and the energy to charge your telephone. This electricity keeps the warm air blowing about your house in the winter. Water pipes bring fresh water. You drink this water, bathe in it, cook with it and water your garden with it. If you have natural gas, it is delivered in pipes as well, keeping you warm, cooking your food and heating your water.

These fragile pipes, wires, and modern roads keep you from a caveman's existence, and that existence is only a few days away in your future if those pipes and wires were to fail. Don't take those wires and pipes for granted. Never assume that they will always be there, and never assume that they will always be working.

Imagine what would happen if some people with the mindset of the New Guinea tribesmen we talked about earlier were to gain control of these wires and pipes. What if they were to employ their delusions to the problem of how to keep the pipes and wires functioning? Imagine the outcome if they were to use the guidance of a possum to determine the maintenance of your local power plant? You think this is not possible?

If so, this is an assumption made possible by your small conceptual radius. Your small conceptual radius was created by your acceptance of the things you learned in the public schools, your church, from the movies, your television and from your parents. Question everything. Think for yourself.

Your modern world depends on the rational thinking of millions of people, and people worldwide are abandoning reason and turning to delusional thinking.

You are in danger in many other ways. Physical reality is a threat to your life twenty-four hours per day. At this very moment, for example, your immune system is fighting infectious microbes and errant cells that pose a threat to your life.

Millions of years ago, a star exploded in our galaxy and the cosmic rays created by this explosion are racing towards Earth. This star possibly has your death sentence written in its ultimate actions. Sometime in the next minutes, one of these cosmic rays will penetrate your body and damage the DNA in one of your cells. Hopefully, your immune system will recognize this damaged cell, race into action and send warrior T-cells to kill that cell. If your immune system does not recognize the errant cell, this cell may divide many times into a cancerous mass that can lead to your death.

You are inhaling bacteria at this very moment. Microbes are standing by to enter any wound you might have. Microbes are on your food. Your mouth alone has millions of bacteria, some of which are deadly and must be kept at a minimum by your immune system. Your body is in a constant war with these threats. Your immune system is at war while you mindlessly watch television and believe everything you hear on the news.

Earth's weather is largely unpredictable. You can be caught in a snowstorm, frigid conditions, a tornado or flood. Earthquakes have killed millions. Hurricanes and cyclones have killed millions. A cyclone that hit Bangladesh in 1970 killed 500,000 people.

Not only do microbes kill people, microbes attack the food you hold in storage. In the 1840s a water mold, *Phytophthora infestans*, a plant pathogen, attacked the stored Irish potato crop and the resulting famine killed one million people. A fungal disease of wheat known as black stem rust, caused by the fungus *Puccinia graminis*, has caused famines since the Roman times, and is still causing famines in our modern world. Famines caused by weather, plant pathogens, insects and governments have wiped out hundreds of millions.

Sometime in the next few hours or days, if you can spare a few moments away from your television, social life, cell phone or computer, you ought to think about the big picture. The big picture will paint for you a scene of danger. You are under pressure at all times, and much of this pressure is hidden from your view.

Starvation is very common to human history. War, disease and natural disasters also erase millions of lives. Your safety is not automatic. You are under attack. Think it over.

You are very weak physically. You see your favorite athletes as being super strong heroes, but they are nothing but total wimps when compared to any animal that has evolved for millions of years to engage in physical battle. Your 200-pound sports hero would be torn to shreds by a 40-pound wolverine. A super heavyweight world champion wrestler would be a pathetic foe for an average silverback gorilla that could easily dispatch your hero in a few seconds.

Humans are physically weak and vulnerable. Without clothes, you are cold at 60 degrees Fahrenheit and hot at 95. Only a very small area of the Earth is suitable for humans who don't have clothing. Even then, the warm, equatorial regions of the Earth have offsetting dangers. You would need protection against biting insects and poisonous plants. You would need shoes to protect your feet. In arid regions, the sun would be relentless and clothing would be mandatory to avoid sunscald so severe that death would be inevitable.

You are slow. Your favorite Olympic track star could easily be chased down and killed by a middle-aged and overweight leopard or tiger. You need food, but the great majority of plants are poisonous. In fact, there are more than 300,000 species of plants, and you would be hard-pressed to find 300 out of the 300,000 that are edible.

Something you were never taught in public schools: *Plants are organisms that manufacture defensive poisons to kill, incapacitate or disorient anything that might eat them.*

Plants can't run. If they were not armed with chemical defenses, animals would quickly multiply to such an extent that most plants would be wiped out of existence.

The green plants you see in your landscape — the maples, oaks, pines, azaleas, pines, locusts, privets, willows, etc., and all the natural weeds, streamside plants, desert plants, etc. — all of these have carbohydrates, vitamins and proteins. These are land plants with which we are all familiar, from the smallest moss to the redwoods. All of these plants have nutrients that are beneficial to human life. However, there is a problem, a big problem: Most likely, less than 2% of these plants are safe for you to eat.[8] The reason for this is because plants make poisons to protect their own lives.

This fact is absolutely essential knowledge for all humans. However, realize that the majority of high school and college graduates have no idea of this basic and most important fact that has impacted humans since humans have existed on Earth. This speaks of the public schools.

In the 1970s, hundreds of thousands of Cambodians died of starvation during a famine. Cambodia is a tropical jungle with billions of plants, and these plants contain nutrients that can sustain human life. The problem is, these nutrients are combined with poisons manufactured by the plants, making the jungle inedible.

Another weakness you face, when compared to other animals, is your ability to obtain food, and your inability to exist without tools. If you want to eat another animal, you will be hard-pressed to chase it down on foot, sneak up on it and catch it by hand, or enter into direct combat.

You need tools to collect your food. You will need a spear or a digging tool, you must fashion a trap or net, or a fishing line. You will need to start a fire to cook your food, as your immune system is not suited to battle the microbes that exist in physical reality. You will need clothes and shoes. Your mammal relative, the wolverine, can dig with his hands in a manner you could never hope to match. A mountain lion can kill a deer without tools. You do not have the ability to live without tools or clothes.

Another disadvantage you have when compared to other animals: You need to gain knowledge. Most life forms don't need to gain knowledge; they are equipped at birth with instincts and a specialized physicality for the battle against physical reality. Many higher animals need to gain some skills, but humans need to gain the most. You are not born with the knowledge of how to plant seeds, make a bow and arrow, or build a shelter.

You are up against physical reality. You are under attack, or will be under attack by some or all of these and more: microbes, cosmic rays, the weather, hunger, earthquakes, floods, animals and other humans.

The primary point here is that you must engage physical reality in order to overcome the problems you face in the real world. You must have clothes, a shelter, food, tools and knowledge. All of this takes work, productive work.

4
Your Biology of Dependence

You can't make it on your own.

There is myth held by many who espouse freedom. This idea is the myth of "the self-made man." The fictional character of John Galt, or the industrial characters of Andrew Carnegie and Henry Ford are examples.

Of course, these men were great men in fiction or real life, but they were not self- made.

The fact is, you do need help from others. John Galt must have had a mother to feed and clothe him. Ford needed the cooperation from his workers and customers, and Carnegie built his empire by expanding on the knowledge developed by countless generations before him.

You had a parent or parents to bring your life into existence. You had care as a baby and as a young person. You needed help in order to learn to read. Many skills were passed on to you from your parents and teachers, from your friends and surroundings.

Strictly speaking, you can make it on your own, just not very well. For example, a newborn baby could stay alive for a few minutes or hours, depending on the conditions. A seven-year-old might make it for weeks or even much longer if surrounded by ideal conditions of weather and food and water availability.

But in the real world, you need the most important aspect of any society: the skills of others.

You can't know everything, and this is the importance of trade. If you spend much of your life learning to become a fine jeweler or artist, a doctor or farmer, you will some day need the skills of a dentist, plumber or steel maker.

Being a specialist, even if your specialty is physical labor, has immeasurable benefits to your life. You will benefit greatly by knowing just one or a few skills and trading those skills to someone who will offer their skill in return.

Suppose you have spent many years learning the skill of grafting and raising fruit trees. To do a good job and offer quality results requires many hours of practice at grafting and many years of growing experience. Someone working as a plumber in a city is not likely to know much about growing cherry trees, so naturally you can give him a tree if he agrees to replace your kitchen sink.

What you are doing here is exchanging your skill of tree-growing with his skill of plumbing. You are exchanging your life force with the plumber's life force. This exchange is biological in nature. The fundamental nature of exchange is best explained by biology, not economics.

Your exchange with the plumber is basic barter, and this barter improves both your lives. Basic barter underpins all exchange, even complex financial transactions, and all of these acts are acts made by biological entities that improve life.

It is possible, after you have had some protection and training by others, that you could leave your parents or guardians at a young age, say 18, go out into the wilderness and build a shelter, make your own clothes, hunt or grow your own food, and live for a time, possibly until old age.

However, you would not have the same degree of safety and comfort you would have if you were to specialize in one skill and trade that skill with others who specialize as well. A bone fracture could mean death, a small cut could lead to a deadly infection, or animals could obliterate your food supply.

Practically speaking, you cannot make it on your own without help as a young person, and you can't make it in old age with comfort and safety without the skills of others, skills you don't have yourself.

5
The Biology of Production

All life forms reshape physical reality.

Trees and other green plants convert the sun's radiation into chemical energy. This is a physical process that changes light (photons) into chemicals that support cell division and growth.

Trees extract moisture, oxygen and mineral nutrients from the soil and the tree's various processes convert these minerals into stored food and new growth. The trees in your backyard or the trees lining your street are engaged in production. They are acting on physical reality and changing this physical reality into chemicals that support their lives.

Herd animals, such as cattle, bison, deer and others, chew and digest grasses and other plants, and their digestive systems convert this botanical material into usable nutrients. These animals are acting on physical reality and are changing existing materials into a different state in order to fuel their lives.

You, or someone working on your behalf, must produce the food you consume, the clothes you wear, the fuel you burn.

You consume other materials twenty-four hours per day. You slowly wear out your bed as you sleep, and you wear out your clothes and shoes daily. For example, assume your bed will last ten years. After 3,650 nights the bed will be worn out and its utility will be consumed. Your socks and shoes, your pants and jacket will wear out in a similar fashion. Every day you consume and wear out production that must be replaced. Your teeth wear down over the years and you will need the productive efforts of a dentist to restore them. If you take excellent care of them you may not need a dentist, but you will have consumed many toothbrushes.

You can't even choose to stop consuming. If you decide to not eat, your body will burn and consume its stored fat. *You consume twenty-four hours per day and you or someone working on your behalf must produce the materials that you consume.* Food, clothing, shelter, fuel, transportation, medicine and many more things are produced for your consumption.

6
The Biology of Storage

You not only rely on production, you, like the trees and bees, must store production for the future. This is true because you consume production twenty-four hours per day, beginning at your conception in your mother's womb until your death. You consume and deplete nutrients while you sleep.

The honey you have with tea or toast comes from bees that made this honey from flower pollen. The bees acted on and changed physical reality into something they could use. A bee colony's honey is food produced and stored by the bees. Flower pollen is not always available to bees, so they must store their production (honey) for later use.

All life forms store production. Even single-celled animals store water and minerals in their cell. Many plants store food in their roots for winter. Plants also store water to see them through times when water is less available.

Various animals collect goods and store them. Squirrels collect nuts and seeds and store them for the winter. Wolves bury animal carcasses and return later for a meal. Owls, spiders, many insects and many more animals store food for winter and lean times.

Resources are scarce for most life forms. Many animals spend their entire day looking for food. Even algae can experience a scarcity of sunlight and exist only in the upper regions of the ocean.

Scarcity is also seasonal. If you grow your own food in any area other than the equatorial regions of the Earth, you must take into consideration the seasons. Many crops will not grow in the winter in cold climates, and in warm climates such as Southern Florida, it may be too warm in the summer months for some vegetable crops. For these reasons food storage is important. For thousands of years, humans have grown crops in favorable seasons and stored the excess production for later consumption when growing is not possible.

Like all life forms, you must produce by changing physical reality and you must store production. Even in the modern world, this still remains a fact regardless of one's occupation.

7
The Biology of Property

It is very easy to demonstrate that most species of animals and plants have a sense of self-ownership. This self-ownership is the basic concept of private property.

We can see this every day. Birds will defend themselves and their nests by attacking intruders. Bees, hornets and wasps will defend their hives by stinging. Crabs will defend themselves and their holes in rocks and coral by attacking trespassers. Some crabs take up residence in empty shells and defend this space with their lives. Most animals will defend their young. Many plants create allopathic chemicals that poison the ground around them in order to protect their real estate. Other plants produce chemicals that poison insects and other animals that might otherwise feed on them. The nicotine in tobacco plants wasn't developed by the tobacco plant to please humans, but rather to poison insects that violate their foliage.

Nicotine produced from tobacco leaves was used in farming as an insecticide for over 200 years.

The alfalfa plant makes a chemical known as medicarpin that inhibits the growth of other alfalfa plants in the same area. By producing this chemical, it is effectively creating private property. Farmers are aware of this process. Once an alfalfa field is established, it is nearly impossible to fill in bare areas by re-seeding. The new seeds will either not germinate, or if they do, the plants will be forever weakened by the defensive chemicals of the older plants. In effect, the older alfalfa plants are saying, "I was here first, this is my property." This process is known as autotoxicity.

Many trees and shrubs manufacture chemicals that suppress the growth of other plants that attempt to invade their space: *Casuarina equisetifolia*, or the Australian pine, *Juglans nigra,* known as black walnut tree, *Salvia leucophylla*, known as purple sage. There are many more, including white rice. This process is known as allelopathy.

Some insects and animals have a community property sense. For example, a wolf pack will defend an area from invasion by other wolves.

Pocket gophers live solitary lives and will even attack their own species to defend property. If another gopher attempts to enter their burrow, an aggressive attack will occur. The examples of self-defense and property defense in nature could take several books to even touch on the subject.

It is obvious that the predisposition towards owning property is common in biology.

8
The Biology of Self-Defense

Self-defense is always a defense of property.

You defend yourself twenty-four hours per day. You couldn't stop this process even if you wanted to, as your immune system is working non-stop to defeat the pathogenic microbes that are forever persistent in their attempts to invade your body.

All plants and animals have developed defense mechanisms. Many cacti are heavily thorned. These thorns deter grazing by animals. The chrysanthemum plant produces the chemical we call pyrethrums. This is an insecticide and is commercially produced from the chrysanthemum plant and sold for use in insecticidal sprays. Of course, the chrysanthemum did not develop this chemical for humans, but rather for its own self-defense.

Other plants and animals use the defense of camouflage to hide their property (their own bodies) from predators.

An interesting feature of the tomato plant is that the plant protects the tomato seed by camouflaging the young fruit by keeping it the same green color as the plant's leaves and stems. Green tomatoes are poisonous, and this attribute offers another layer of protection.

When the seeds are mature, the tomato's fruit turns bright red and loses its toxicity. In essence the plant is communicating, "Here I am, eat me." Another interesting twist is that tomato seeds are transported by tomato-eating animals to another location, thereby gaining distribution.

Notice that you have a very hard time in crushing a tomato seed with your teeth. The seeds are just too slick and rounded. The seeds squirt away from your teeth and you will swallow most of them intact. This has a function, in that tomato seeds will not germinate unless they have been in an acid bath. If a hundred tomato seeds are planted directly from a red, ripe tomato, only a small percentage, if any, will germinate. However, if the seeds have been through an acid bath, a very high percentage of them will germinate. (Packaged tomato seeds have been exposed to acid in order to defeat this germination inhibitor.)

In essence, this is what the tomato plant is communicating: "I'm hiding this green fruit because the seeds are not mature. This green tomato is poisonous!" Later, the plant is signaling: "The seeds are mature. I'm making the fruit bright red and visible. Come eat me and distribute my seeds." Once the animal has eaten the tomato, the seeds will get past the animal's teeth unharmed, get an acid bath in the animal's stomach, and get transported to another area.

This remarkable story of the tomato's actions is instructive. If the tomato could speak, it might say: "This green fruit is mine until I say otherwise. Caution: No trespassing. I will tell you when my private property becomes public property; otherwise, act at your own risk."

The tomato is just one of hundreds of thousands of species of plants, and every species has its own story of defense and survival. These actions by plants and animals are demonstrative of the built-in eloquence of self-preservation found in life.

The skunk uses an odorous gas to repel predators. A poisonous snake will strike in self-defense, and there are thousands of plants that are deadly even to many species of grazing animals that have evolved counter-measures. Plants have spent millions of years evolving chemical defenses that repel foraging animals, including humans. Plants and animals have self-defense mechanisms that have been honed through millions of years of trial and error.

In humans, property is a fundamental aspect of life. This property stems from the fact that you have the choice of thought and you *create* the resulting action.

Thought experiment: Move your thumb. Now move your toes. Now, go outside and stand in the street. It is possible you obeyed the first two commands, but probably not the third. Any choice you may have made, you chose to do so. *It was your choice.* You can choose your actions. You can choose *not* to believe you have a choice, in which case, you prove you do.

This ability to initiate thought and action, and the diversity of the abilities and flavors of cognitive styles in individuals is the core of identity.

You create your thoughts, you create and direct your actions, and you have a built-in sense of ownership. Demonstrative evidence of this ownership is available to you by the observation of nature and the vast quantity of information that proves the point beyond any doubt.

Observation beats theory. Observation is the direct recording of facts as they unfold.

Philosophically, if the idea of ownership is valid, then this validity stems from creation and choice. Because you are the creator of your thoughts, and because you choose to act or not to act, you own the thoughts and resulting actions. However, philosophy is a poor way to validate something as important as self–ownership.

Observation, measurement and experiment always trump the mind-wrenching mental gymnastics of philosophers.

Self-defense, self-ownership, and the genetic drive for owning property are demonstrable facts that can be measured and validated by experiment.

The greatest need for any human seeking to live in a peaceful society is that of long-term and dependable stability in his personal property that we know is an extension of his work and biology.

This long-term stability in property ownership is the foundation of trade and progress. The bedrock, the solid platform of any peaceful society that has made significant progress in the alleviation of human misery, is the broad recognition of self-ownership, the natural propensity for humans to defend themselves, and the observance of the natural occurrence of private property.

9
The Biology of Trade

In our next thought experiment, let us assume that you live in a small community of 100 people. We can start small and make things less complicated. For the moment, let's strip away the politics, the internet, labor unions, the wars, the Federal Reserve, the banking system and international treaties. We won't get involved the multitude of complexities that can fog the real underlying issues that humans face when dealing with each other. In this way, we can reflect on the basic principles involved with human interaction.

Societies start small. The United States started with immigrants crossing the Bering Land Bridge about 12,000 years ago, with settlers from Europe coming later. We have no written record of how many crossed the land bridge coming from the West, but we do know the first Europeans came in small numbers. From these small numbers and immigration, a country of 300 million people has developed.

As we have seen, you cannot make it on your own as a child, and as an adult you cannot make it on your own and live very well. Some day you will need help.

Let us assume you have experience and knowledge of how to grow corn, but know little about how to kill an animal and cure the meat. You also may not know how to bind a book or smelt iron ore. It is very easy to see that you would do well if you grew more corn than you needed and traded some of your excess corn to the hunter for his meat, and some more of your excess corn to the dentist to fix a bad tooth.

Barter is the exchange of goods and services for goods and services. Barter emerges when people specialize in their work.

The most fundamental form of barter is direct labor exchange. For example, you could tend your neighbor's cornfield in exchange for his labor of repairing your roof. In this case, you would be giving your labor to him in exchange for his labor. Even more fundamentally, we can say that you are trading your specialized knowledge for your neighbor's specialized knowledge. This is an important point in that it reveals the underlying essentials of trade. You do not have much knowledge about roofing and your neighbor has little knowledge of growing corn.

If you specialize in growing corn, you will become an expert. You will know more about growing corn than the dentist or shoemaker. At the same time, you will know less about making shoes than the shoemaker, and you will not want to work on your own teeth.

By trading your corn for various products and services in your community, you will gain the expertise of all you trade with. You benefit; they benefit.

Trade gives everyone leverage against the hostile forces of nature. With trade, you are able to more easily defend yourself against the weather, hunger and disease. You can trade your corn for the services of a carpenter to build a shelter, trade for warm clothing and trade for the services of a doctor. *Your expertise in one area gives you access to expertise in all areas.*

In effect, trade gives you a vast pool of knowledge from which you can draw. Simply being an expert at growing corn has gained you the expertise of many people.

Trade is common in nature. Plants trade with other plants and animals, and plants even trade with microbes.

A relationship between two individuals from different species that has a benefit to both individuals is known as a symbiotic relationship.

With every meal, you engage in trade with the billions of microbes in your intestines that process your food for you. Your intestines provide them a good home and they supply you with life-giving nutrients. Mutualistic trade is very common in nature.

The clown fish lives in close proximity to the sea anemone. The clown fish provides a benefit to the anemone by dining on small invertebrates that would otherwise feed on the anemone. The anemone protects the clown fish by producing a toxin that stings other fish. The clown fish is immune to this toxin that the anemone produces. These two species make a perfect pair by making a perfect trade.

The Amazon tree, *Doroia hirsute,* provides nutrients and a home for the ant species *Myrmelachista schumanni.* These ants attack nearby plants that otherwise would be competitors for soil, nutrients, water and light to their host. The ants inject the competitors' leaves with formic acid that kills or suppresses the competition.

Mycorrhizal fungi colonize the roots of over 100,000 species of plants. Plants provide the fungi with carbohydrates and the fungi greatly increase the plant's ability to uptake nutrients. If this relationship of mutual trade ceased to exist, most land animals (including you) would die in a short amount of time.

Trade for mutual benefit is common throughout nature. This process is known as symbiosis.

We have seen some examples of symbiotic relationships. If the individuals are from the same species, we call this an *intraspecies* symbiotic relationship.

An example of the latter would be the behavior of some chimpanzees when they de-flea and groom each other. This behavior is the direct exchange of labor. It is simple barter.

Indirect labor exchange occurs when the exchange of labor is accomplished via physical objects to which labor has been applied. For example, if you traded your corn to a shoemaker for a pair of shoes, this can be considered labor exchange via commodities. The corn has the attributes of your labor, the shoes the attributes of the shoemaker's labor. Hence, you are engaging in an intraspecies symbiotic relationship.

10
The Biology of Money

Some life forms can hold their biological attributes outside their bodies, in other physical forms. A bird's nest, for example, is an external projection of a bird's biology. Many animals build shelters, hollow out the ground, or build sleeping areas.

Some plants have the ability to manufacture allopathic chemicals and deposit them in the soil. Allopathic chemicals are herbicides. They act as plant growth inhibitors. These allopathic chemicals are produced by some species of plants in order to retard the growth of other plant species that would otherwise be their competition. Walnut trees do this, as do many other species of plants.

One could rightfully make the judgment that these allopathic chemicals in the soil around a walnut tree are part of the tree's biology, even though the chemicals are not physically connected to the tree itself. In fact, if the walnut tree were to die and then be removed, the allopathic chemicals remaining in the soil would still be a feature of the walnut tree's biology. We could then correctly conclude that these chemicals are leftover production from the tree.

The point here is that many species change their environment and create products that are external to their bodies, but are nevertheless biological attributes of the entities themselves.

We can see this in a beehive. The bees collect nectar from flowers, and in a complicated process, use enzymes and regurgitation to process the nectar into honey. Their purpose is to produce honey as a stored food source. This honey is stored in their hive and provides the bees food in the winter months, the period when flowers and therefore nectar are not available.

If this honey is removed, placed in a jar, and delivered to your breakfast table, the honey can be correctly classified as a feature of bee biology. It is accumulated bee production.

Animals produce and store production outside their bodies. Humans do this as well.

Returning to our thought experiment of the last chapter, assume you have grown so much corn that the marketplace cannot take all of your corn when it is ready in the fall. At this point you can decide to store your excess production.

You then process this excess production. It now displays your biological attributes in that, you grew the corn, you shucked the corn and you stored the corn. The corn now has distinct characteristics of your biological effort and energy: It is condensed, it is shucked and dried, and it is protected from moisture and other animals.

Just as honey does not exist in nature without the action of bees, corn that has been processed in the above manner does not exist without human action. As honey has the biological attributes of bees, this corn, your accumulated production, has the attributes of your work. It is an extension of your biology. It is your stored biological energy, your stored production, your stored labor.

Further assume you need a new pair of boots, but the shoemaker has plenty of corn for his current needs. This problem is known as the "coincidence of wants." If your need for boots does not coincidentally match the shoemaker's need for corn, you may not make a trade. However, assume the shoemaker knows that corn is in general demand and not everyone is overstocked, and that he also knows that dried corn will last a year or more. He then might trade with you knowing that he can exchange the corn for other goods at another time.

Now suppose that your shoemaker needs more leather from the local hunter, but the hunter does not need new shoes. The shoemaker might trade corn for more leather, that is, if the hunter believes the corn will be exchangeable in the future.

At this point, the corn has become money.

"Money is a commonly traded commodity that is used as a vehicle for the exchange of stored labor."[9]

Most importantly, when you trade, you trade your biological attributes. Trade is the exchange of biological energy. You trade your energy and specialty of growing corn for the shoemaker's energy and specialty of making boots.

Money is the storage of biological energy and the means of exchanging biological energy while avoiding the problem of the coincidence of wants. Your corn has in effect carried your biological energy and the attributes of your biology into the marketplace and made this energy fungible.

Assume your community of one hundred people grows into a small country of a few thousand. Assume someone discovers metals, iron, copper, etc. In time, corn will fall from favor as money because metals will hold a higher concentration of human energy.

The quality of money

Many things can be and have been money. The quality of money is an important question and concerns rarity, stability, storability, acceptability and portability.

Corn is not very stable. It can be attacked by insects, rodents, fungal diseases and bacteria. It is difficult to store long-term because it must be kept dry, cool and pest free, and will degrade with time. Salt has been money, but it is corrosive and must be kept dry. Salt is also relatively abundant in some areas and is not rare enough to warrant transporting large quantities to serve as a labor storage device.

It is easy to see that a paper note can be a money substitute. Suppose in your community of 100 people, the market barters with a paper note known as a "Corn Unit." A corn farmer could print these paper receipts and title them as such. His reasoning could be that he would guarantee the delivery of corn in exchange for the notes. For example, if a person has a "10 Corn Unit" paper note, the farmer would gladly exchange 10 bushels of corn for the note, on demand. As long as the corn farmer remains honest, and as long as he prints a quantity of notes that does not exceed his inventory of stored corn, everything will run smoothly.

When you deliver to the market some carrots, your customer could give you a number of paper Corn Unit notes in exchange. You could then exchange these units for other goods, save the notes for a rainy day, or visit your shoemaker who most likely has heard of the Corn Units and might be willing to accept them in exchange for a pair of boots.

What would be the *quality* of these market units? Well, they have little intrinsic value. They might be used to start a fire or as toilet paper, but surely a handful of paper is not worth a cartload of corn. However, it is possible that the short-term quality of these Corn Units could be very high. To remain a quality money, the producer of the Corn Units must be totally honest, because if he is not, then he could just print all the Corn Units he desires and flood the community with paper and purchase goods with actual intrinsic value. In this way, he could enrich himself at the expense of everyone else. So then, another attribute of quality money is that, *its value must be independent of promises.*

Eventually, because of the above problems with many commodities, precious metals will become the favorable vehicle for the storage and exchange of labor. This is a natural evolutionary consequence of free trade and market forces. This evolution has occurred throughout human history, even when cultures have been isolated.

Government money

Money is not a creation of government. In fact, money is the naturally occurring result of exchange. As trade evolves, it is only natural that those who exchange will gravitate toward those methods that require less effort.

This constant search for easier ways of doing things will lead to a type of money that minimizes the efforts required to solve the labor-intensive problem of the "coincidence of wants." It is difficult to dig with one's hands, so invent a shovel; it is difficult to carry bushels of corn around, so make copper, silver or gold coins.

After the natural forces of trade prompted humans to use commodities as money, governments moved in to exploit this situation by force and symbolism. The theft that followed is quite possibly the greatest fraud ever conceived.

Humans involved in non-violent trade invented money.

Governments did not invent money. Governments only created and perpetuated the myth that money was invented by government. Governments have sustained this myth by the fostering and maintenance of this grand delusion. For more on money, see the addendum.

11
The Psychology of Trust

The expectation of *truthfulness* dominates a successful society based of self-ownership. The expectation of *lies and deception* dominates a society based on the erasure of self-ownership.

Trust is a condition found in nature. Sheep learn to trust the guard dog, the Great Pyrenees, to live among them as a protector. Cleaner fish clean the mouths and teeth of predator fish such as the grouper and even sharks. This biological behavior is known as mutualism. Trust between humans stems from the mutual recognition of self-ownership.

The expectation of the truth being told is the lubricant of successful trade. Without this atmosphere of trust, trade becomes strained, and the costs rise for all involved. Trade is the means by which you gain the biological attributes of others; the alternative to trade is violence or trickery.

In another thought experiment, assume you have grown corn and wish to make an exchange with the miller who produces ground wheat or flour.

Suppose you deliver a cartload of corn, unload the cart, and the miller refuses to give you the flour. You could threaten him with force and he might return the threat, or might even have his armed family waiting in the wings. It is easy to see that the threat or assumption of violence can be a great barrier to trade. If this state of affairs were common in a society, trade would break down and your ability to gain the talents of others would be diminished.

We can see these problems in the drug trade and other underworld endeavors. Where governments have made free trade illegal, trust is diminished and violence is the expectation.

Assume you grow marijuana, and that it is perfectly legal to do so. You harvest your marijuana and wish to sell it in the marketplace. Is there any reason that the selling of marijuana ought to be more violent than the sale of corn?

Moreover, suppose the sale of marijuana is illegal and brings a prison term. Further assume armed government agents routinely go undercover to catch those who sell marijuana illegally, and that their intent is to take you as a prisoner. This is where the violence is introduced and trust is broken. You may decide to get out of the marijuana business or employ countermeasures. You no longer trust anyone. You expect to be lied to. Your customers don't trust you, as you might be a government agent. Some of your customers might arm themselves and enter into every transaction with the premise that a shoot-out is better than prison. Notice the violence in the 1920s during prohibition. When alcohol was illegal, violence ensued; when alcohol became legal again, the violence dropped.

Now, assume you visit your local food store and purchase a five-dollar loaf of bread and hand the cashier a one-hundred-dollar bill. Assume the cashier claims you gave him a twenty-dollar bill. Further assume this is common in the community you live in. Imagine the problems involved. You must now double and triple check everything you do. You constantly worry that your garden will be looted at night. You worry about your house being robbed.

A generalized assumption that the truth will be told and honesty will prevail is the psychological foundation of trade. You must, as you promised, give a full bushel of quality corn to your local electrician in exchange for repairing the wiring in your house. You are unlikely to know that the wiring he is using might be substandard and can cause a fire; he is unlikely to know that the corn might have a mold that can cause illness.

If you desire a society where humans are free of violence, that is to say, where private property is the standard, you must be honest in your dealings with people. Successful self-ownership requires honesty in trade.

The expectation of *dishonesty* dominates any society based on the erasure of self-ownership and property. The history of countries that have erased the idea of private property is the history of misery and deception on a grand scale. Nazi Germany, Nazi Italy, Imperial Japan, the Soviet Union, communist China under Mao, communist Cambodia, North Korea - all of these regimes expropriated human lives and property in order to fuel the state. These societies lived under a continuous cloud of deception and lies as government propaganda rained down from above. Trust evaporated. Sons reported their fathers, daughters reported their mothers, and sisters turned against brothers. A billion people were afraid of speak the truth.

It has been said many times that "money is the medium of exchange." This is untrue. Exchange is possible without money. If the expectation of truth and goodwill dominates a community, the benefits of trade are realized to the greatest extent. Trade is your life-force multiplier. Trust and non-violence, or to put it more directly, trust that there will be no violence, is the lubricant of trade. This is the real "medium of exchange." Trade happens when the middle ground is trust.

In societies where trust is not dominant, for example, in the drug trades or the prohibition era in the United States, violence is expected and there is a price to pay, in that, the expectation of violence produces a risk premium. For example, marijuana by the pound is roughly 1,000 times more expensive than apples, 2,000 times more expensive than potatoes.

The cost to grow marijuana is no greater than the cost to grow apples, that is, if marijuana were not illegal. The expectation of violence is the driver behind the high price —not only violence from dealer to dealer and dealer to customer, but the risk of government violence while enforcing drug laws.

The tack of trust is detrimental to free trade and a free society.

12
The Biology of Intraspecies Predation and Kleptoparasitism

Predation is the act of severely wounding or killing for physical or psychological gain. Kleptoparasitism is the act of stealing the product of another's labors.

You face these two problems daily. In reference to predation, if you live in the wilderness, you might be the subject of a lion or bear attack, where these animals intend to make you a meal or eliminate you as a threat. If you live in a city, you might be the subject of a killer who desires a human trophy. If you live in a country such as Nazi Germany, the Soviet Union, or Mao's Communist China, you will constantly face the threat of predation, as human on human predation is the official policy of systems such as these.

You certainly face the problem of kleptoparasitism. Klepto means "theft," and we all know parasitism means that one organism feeds on and benefits at the expense of another. Hence: "parasitism by theft." An example of a kleptoparasite would be your neighbor when he steals your corn in the middle of the night.

In all cases, only one side benefits. You grew the corn. You bought the seeds with your money, which you now know is your labor, you expended the labor to plant the seeds, you bought or rented your property paid for by your labors, you bought the fertilizer. You expended your life force to grow the corn, but now your neighbor has turned to kleptoparasitism in order to avoid the effort of farming.

Kleptoparasitism is common. A lion will make a kill and the hyenas will move in to rob the lion. A bird will dig for a worm, and another bird will dive in to steal it.

It is less common for animals of the same species to engage in this behavior. However, it does happen. This is known as intraspecies kleptoparasitism.

Few species resort to this tactic, and when they do, it is seldom a major or primary source of resources. For example, when a lion makes a kill, other lions may join in on the meal at their own risk. Scrimmages may take place. In most cases of intraspecies kleptoparasitism, the animal will defend its property and sometimes do so to the death of one of the actors. As we have seen, production (property) is an extension of animal and human biology, so defense of property is actually self-defense. The lion that made the kill is defending his expended labor or biological energy.

When human intraspecies kleptoparasitism is non-existent, this state of affairs is known as freedom. Freedom is nothing more than being free of intraspecies kleptoparasitism and intraspecies predation.

When intraspecies kleptoparasitism and intraspecies predation are the official policies of a government, we call this system socialism, communism, fascism, or a monarchy and this is the general state of affairs we live in today.

(*There was a brief period in the United States when these human conditions or diseases were minimal — the early years of American history. In fact, the US Constitution was written in such a way as to outlaw intraspecies kleptoparasitism and intraspecies predation. However, the framers of the Constitution did not write it based on biology; rather, they based the document on the erroneous doctrine of natural rights. Without a factual and logical foundation, the Constitution was doomed to erosion and eventual failure.*

This failure was assured when the Left found the underlying weakness in the doctrine of natural rights. The way they exploited this weakness was to drown it by dilution. New rights were created, such as women's rights, gay rights, health care rights, animal rights and many more. With all of these new rights, many of which were purposefully ridiculous, the natural rights as proposed by the Founding Fathers were lost in a soup of outrageous claims. Since the doctrine of "the unalienable rights of man" is nothing more than a vacant, emotionally based wish logically equivalent to any right one can imagine, the system was conceptually defenseless.)

One jackal or hyena will move toward a lion's meal; the lion lunges at the kleptoparasite while another hyena sneaks in from the other side. The same applies when your neighbor steals your corn, he will wait until you are not at home or wait till the dark of night. *Kleptoparasitism almost always involves trickery.*

The tricks politicians use to engage in intraspecies kleptoparasitism are a slight of hand of another type; actually, we should call it a "slight of mind." These mental tricks are made possible by your acceptance of the delusional thoughts we talked about in Chapter 2. Politicians work very hard to reinforce these delusions.

First, you most likely have accepted the idea of original sin. From the beginning, you were disarmed. Your internal core was compromised, in that, your sense of being a good person that ought to stand up for your own nature, the nature that gives you property and the predisposition to defend that property, was weakened. You also accepted the false premise that you were not natural to this Earth. Without giving it much thought, you probably believe you have a duty towards others, a social contract. This is a huge burden. Philosophers, religions, kings and governments have driven these falsehoods and propaganda into the minds of billions.

After you accept these delusions as being fact, your natural predisposition to create, use and defend your property is diminished. You no longer have the conceptual high ground. You are conceptually defenseless.

Unlike a lion that will attack any kleptoparasite that attempts to take his food, you don't have instincts to tell you what to do. Imagine a slick politician telling a lion that he is not natural to this Earth, that he is soaked in original sin, that he has a duty to some government and that he ought to turn over his zebra hind quarter. No doubt, the politician would be gutted in short order. The lion, by his instinct, automatically knows what to do to protect his life and property. You need to learn.

Religion teaches that you are a sinner at birth. Environmentalists teach you that you are not natural to this planet, and the politicians tell you that you have a duty to others, a duty that demands you submit to intraspecies kleptoparasitism. All three of these notions that have been accepted by you are delusions; they are tricks. Your blind acceptance of these tricks opens the door for the jackals and hyenas.

Just like millions of other species of life on Earth, you must change nature and produce, you must store this production, and you must defend this production from the elements and parasites, regardless of the type of parasite: microbial, animal or other humans.

13
The Property Sanction

Human life is enhanced by the division of labor and the exchange of that labor. A peaceful and thriving community is propagated when labor exchange is based on the biologically imposed presumption of self-ownership and private property. The medium through which this trade moves is the presumption of the truth being told and non-violence.

> Let us not forget that the cultivation of the earth
> is the most important labor of man.
> When tillage begins, other arts follow.
> The farmers, therefore, are the founders of civilization.
> - Daniel Webster

Unlike hunting or gathering, agriculture requires that the producer remain in one place for a length of time. Even fast crops take two or three months to produce. It takes years for fruit and nut trees to mature.

In a hunting-and-gathering culture, you are subject to extremes of weather. Grains may be plentiful in one year, but not the next. A drought might devastate the fish population in one year and floods might devastate tree fruits the next. With agriculture, you can store excess production in good years and have a supply in the bad years.

A prerequisite for agriculture, beyond good growing conditions, is the idea of private property. This is fundamental in that a farmer cannot watch his crops twenty-four hours per day to guard against thieves.

(You might object and float the idea that collective farms are possible. They are possible, and in fact, grand experiments involving hundreds of millions of people over a seventy-year time period in the Soviet Union and communist China prove that a government-forced policy of collective farming propagates famine and the deaths of millions.)

Without this atmosphere, the atmosphere of private property being respected, no farmer would attempt to grow beyond his immediate and personal needs. The risk of theft would be too great and the security on a large piece of land too extensive.

This atmosphere of honesty, trust and respect for property is necessary for a healthy agrarian culture. Without a respect for property, a crowd of people would take your corn before you could harvest it. *Your* goal would be to harvest the corn at its peak of quality in order to maximize your return on investment, the investment of seed, fertilizer and your own labor, the cost of which is your lost opportunity in other endeavors. Thieves would be content to steal the corn at a lower point in quality, as they would have nothing invested, so optimal timing would be of little importance to them.

If the thieves were successful, the following year you would grow only a small amount of corn, the amount you could personally defend, and you would be forced to harvest early and very frequently. You would have little left to barter; therefore, the lack of respect for property leads to the loss of trade. A successful farm cannot exist in a den of thieves.

So far you have seen that to have a life you must produce and store excess production. To have a better life you need to specialize and trade your specialty. In order to make trade possible you need trust and an atmosphere of honesty. Finally, you need to have others respect your self-ownership, which is, your body and your production.

In order to gain trust and live a non-contradictory life, you must grant others the promise that you will not violently infringe on their lives. This means you will not use force or violence on their property. You must grant this promise to others and hope for the best in that they grant this promise to you.

To recap, one's property is one's body and the biological attributes of one's labor that has been applied to physical reality. As we have seen, this property is a genetic reality. We can easily see this reality in a multitude of species from plants to animals; it is the natural course of events.

We can call this promise a sanction. In effect, by offering a property sanction, you are granting this promise to all the seven billion people on the planet. This act seems minute on the surface, but in fact, it is very important. You have done the right thing in that you recognize that humans, like thousands of other life forms, have a property sense or property gene, and you must not use violence, poison or trickery to gain the possession of their property. This sanction is a gift to others, but in reality, the greatest benefit is to yourself. In a society free of intraspecies predation, your life will be enhanced by the low cost of trade, and trade is the life force multiplier.

With this sanction, this promise, you are living like many other species. Even vicious animals like wolves and hyenas live with little intraspecies parasitism. With the exception of instinctively driven mating rituals, most of the animal world lives in a world of non-violence within their own species. The super predator, the Alaskan brown bear, normally a solitary animal, exists in relative peace with other bears while fishing the streams in summer. They gather in numbers and scrimmage for property on the streams and then go about their lives with little violence.

With this sanction, you are making a stand to forgo theft and violence. You are refusing to be an intraspecies parasite or predator. Your gift to the rest of your species is now fully understood by you, and *this gift is the most valuable gift you can bestow on the human race.*

14
You Against Government

Governments are created and manned by psychopaths,
as government makes an ideal outlet for their perversions.

"Mao issued order after order berating provincial cadres
for being too soft, and urged more "massive arrests, massive killings." On 23 January 1951, for instance, he criti-
cized one province for 'being much too lenient, and not
killing [enough]'; when it raised its execution rate, he said
this improvement made him feel 'very delighted.' "[9a]

As soon as some well-meaning and honest people get together to address
a way to fix a minor problem, those prone to manipulation and deception

will turn the minor problem into a major problem, and then snake their way into holding the reigns of power and create a government or advance the power of an existing government. Those who con, deceive, manipulate and have little remorse are known as psychopaths.*

Once in power, their deviousness is never-ending. They must continuously invent new falsehoods in order to maintain a delusional mindset in the population. They must create a threat internally or externally. Great enemies must be invented, foreign or domestic. The enemies can be terrorism, poverty, drugs, alcohol, global warming, Jews, tobacco, pollution, cancer; the list is unending. The trick is to take a small problem or non-problem and make it a *great* problem. There must be a *war* on terror, a *war* on drugs, a *war* on poverty, or a *war* on cancer. Psychopaths in governments are in a constant race to invent predicaments that dwarf the individual and justify a totalitarian state.

Another ruse is that of grandiosity. We must have a Great Wall, a Great Pyramid or travel to the moon. These great feats are nothing more than a way to openly make the individual feel small while covertly making the government bigger. How can *one* person dare to object to going to the moon or building a Great Pyramid?

Another dwarfing mechanism is to fabricate magnificent entities that can only exist via delusional thinking, for example, the "collective" or the "environment." These delusional concepts are not easily deconstructed by the average mind. The master illusionists therefore deceive the people into giving away their lives and freedoms.

Then there is war. The average Iranian or North Korean has no reason to hate an American. The average American has little reason to hate anyone from another country. A German in 1930 had little reason to hate

---

* Dr. Robert Hare who has spent decades in the study of psychopaths (see his book in the recommended list) refers to them as "intraspecies predators." In the documentary film *Fishhead*, speaking of psychopaths, he states, "is a person without a conscience, have a stunning lack of empathy, an ability to look at people as mere objects, extremely egotistical, self-centered, lacking remorse for what they have done – they are manipulating and are deceiving people for their own ends."

a Jewish storeowner. A North Korean farmer, if lacking the delusional mindset produced by the propaganda of the North Korean dictatorship, would no doubt relish the prospect of sitting down with an American farmer to discuss farming ideas. This is also true in reverse. Sincere people who honestly live by their nature have no hatred. Governments (and some religions) push the hatred of one group towards another. They need a reason for war, and war gives them power over you and your wallet.

As you now know, humans, like thousands of other species, have a propensity to own and protect property, a "property gene" if you will, and this tendency for individual sovereignty runs counter to the desires of the predators. They see this as bad thinking. This bad thinking, thinking that includes the natural motivation to produce, store and defend property, is the antithesis to all their desires, and they must control this troublesome feature of human nature. Most importantly, they must keep their victims in a delusional state. One method of correcting this bad thinking is re-education camps, where the victims are herded into squalid locations and forced into brutal labor and tortured.

In an article about the Vietnamese reeducation camps:

"Hung Huy Nguyen, 71, along with an estimated 1 million South Vietnamese, is a man who came to know death and torture in the years following a war that tore apart families, countries, generations.

His was a world where friends died suddenly. Violently. Where others slowly wasted away from malnutrition and disease. Where stealing a grain of rice led to lashes on the back, down bony legs. Where men and women silently endured, night after night, grasping at hope that someday they might see their children again.

There are no official figures on how many prisoners were executed or how many died from poor treatment. There are no known government records of who was sent to the "re-education" camps, or for how long. There are no archives on the jails, or of what went on. Such are the ways of war, and the treatment of those on the losing side.

A four-month review by the Register of these camps, however, shows a widespread pattern of neglect, persecution and death for tens of thousands of Vietnamese who fought side by side with American soldiers.

To corroborate the experiences of refugees now living in Orange County, the Register interviewed dozens of former inmates and their families, both in the United States and Vietnam; analyzed hundreds of pages of documents, including testimony from more than 800 individuals sent to jail; and interviewed Southeast Asian scholars. The review found:

- An estimated 1 million people were imprisoned without formal charges or trials.

- 165,000 people died in the Socialist Republic of Vietnam's re-education camps, according to published academic studies in the United States and Europe.

- Thousands were abused or tortured: their hands and legs shackled in painful positions for months, their skin slashed by bamboo canes studded with thorns, their veins injected with poisonous chemicals, their spirits broken with stories about relatives being killed.

- Prisoners were incarcerated for as long as 17 years, according to the U.S. Department of State, with most terms ranging from three to 10 years.

- At least 150 re-education prisons were built after Saigon fell 26 years ago."[9b]

This is the price you may pay for "bad thinking." Mao Zedong murdered 70 million people, a conservative number; some believe this number is much higher. Stalin murdered over 30 million.[10] These numbers exclude deaths by war. These numbers are internal deaths, political murders. In an effort to purge bad thinking, regimes eliminate whole groups of people. Hitler killed the Jews. The Russian communists killed the businessmen. Mao killed millions of farmers. These killings have one goal: the elimination of the thinking that holds that individuals are sovereign, that they own themselves.

Once a society sets down the path of oppressive government, where the government is considered the source of "social justice" and income equality, the psychopaths work their way to the top of the heap. Their success is brought about by the ignorance of the population in general. The citizens fall for the propaganda as the psychopaths know exactly how to prey on their irrational delusions. The politicians eventually gain ultimate power due to little resistance. After all, the thought is: *Humans are defective at birth; they aren't even natural to this Earth; they are greedy because they want to keep the fruits of their labor. Someone has to control them.*

Like a wolf that can sense fear, a politician can sense your weaknesses. Your major weakness is your propensity for holding delusions. *Man is the delusional animal.* Rid yourself of delusions, and you will have no mental weaknesses the predators can exploit.

15
Some Economic Myths

This chapter is not intended to unequivocally disprove all of the economic myths that exist. Rather, this is only a sampling of a style of thinking that is necessary for you to conceptually punch through the fog that obscures the real issues. Refer to the list of books in the recommended reading list at the end of this book to gain a deeper understanding.

The pie is a limited size.

In a system based on private property, the pie is unlimited. You make your own pie; you don't need to lust after what is not yours. The harder and smarter you work, the more you gain. Take a look at the size of the economy of the United States in 1800, in 1900 and then in 1950. During these 150 years, Americans were relatively free to pursue their own interests and, for the most part, their property was protected by law. Under these conditions, the pie grew larger and the average standard of living grew along with that pie.

Another's success is stolen from you.

This is a twist on the above belief that the pie is fixed. If your neighbor invents a widget that sells millions, his fortune has nothing to do with your misfortunes. This is easily provable by assuming your neighbor never existed. If he never existed and never invented his widget, would you now be richer? Another question: If your neighbor were a very good swimmer, would your swimming improve if he were to become paralyzed?

Government can create jobs.

Governments can only move jobs around; government does not create net increases in job numbers. This is another slight-of-hand trick klepto-parasites use, and it works like this: Suppose the government taxes everyone $1,000 and builds a large factory that employs 10,000. You can see the 10,000 people going to work every day. The politicians make sure the cameras are trained on the factory entrance and the happy employees give glowing interviews to the television reporters. Thousands of new homes are built near the new factory and hundreds of carpenters, plumbers and roofers are employed. Wow! The government has created all these jobs, you think. These jobs are easy to see.

However, there are millions of little things you can't see or just never observe. Mr. and Mrs. Jones and thousands of other families had planned on buying a new washing machine this year, but their loss of income due to the $1,000 in tax makes this impossible. The washing machine manufacturers dismiss hundreds of employees.

Several thousand other people planned on buying new cars, but because of the new taxes, they can't afford to. The automobile factories dismiss thousands of workers. Millions of people now eat out less, and thousands of restaurants reduce the working hours of dishwashers, waitresses and managers. Thousands of jobs are lost one at the time. A few thousand miners are dismissed at a few iron ore mines and steel mills because the orders are smaller from the washing machine and auto manufactures. Towns suffer, homes are lost to foreclosure, and mechanics, dentists, doctors and carpenters are all affected with less income.

All of these government-created jobs happen at once. The television stations and newspapers cover the event with enthusiasm. However, the job *losses* are unreported or given little coverage, simply because they are scattered throughout the country.

Minimum wage laws and high regulation create better working conditions.

Here is another revealing thought experiment. The current federal minimum wage, as this is being written, is $7.25 per hour. Many argue that the minimum wage ought to be raised.

Assume the wage is raised to $100 per hour. At this rate it is quite easy to see that fast food restaurants, factories, retail stores and many other business would need to dismiss millions of people. If the minimum wage were then lowered to $95 per hour, a few people might be hired back. If the minimum wage were then lowered to $90 per hour, a few more might be rehired.

Now, for your thought experiment: Assume the minimum wage is lowered daily from $100 by $1 per hour. It is quite easy to see that with each lowering a few would be rehired. Once the wage returned to its previous level of $7.25, employment would return to its previous level. Now assume it is lowered to $6 per hour, then $5, then $3, then $2 and then to 0. It is easy to see that many businesses would now hire teenagers, old people, low-skilled workers, etc. Minimum wage laws create unemployment. Minimum wage laws also drive employers to automate. Once wages become more expensive than automation, workers are fired and machines replace them.

Imagine you own a small business, let's say, an accounting office. You have two employees and must do a lot of the work yourself because you can't afford another employee. You stress all week getting the mail out, answering emails and working the spreadsheets. Not only that — you must pull weeds in your garden and mow your lawn every Saturday, take your children to school activities, etc. Would you not be willing to pay an unskilled teen $3 per hour to answer your phones? Sure, most would.

The teen would gain experience in the physical world, he would stay off the streets for a few hours per week, and he would gain self-respect.

Of course, the barrier to all of this is the minimum wage law and the regulations involved. You not only must pay him $7.25 per hour, you will be held responsible for his health and welfare. There are thousands of pages of law concerning this type of hiring and you will have little knowledge of how to comply with all of these laws, and will possibly face fines and penalties for giving the boy some work.

Government workers contribute to the government's income through taxation.

Millions of government workers undoubtedly believe they contribute to the government by paying income taxes.

Assume Mary works for the Federal Department of Transportation. She makes $6,000 per month and the government withholds $1,000 per month federal income tax. Her net pay is therefore $5,000. She fully believes she is paying her taxes and pulling her weight. Not true.

To expand on this, assume a new law is passed where federal workers are not required to pay federal income tax. Now, Mary receives $5,000 dollars per month without any tax withheld. In terms of finance, nothing has changed. The government is still out a net $5,000 per month, and Mary Jones still earns her $5,000. Therefore, withholding "income tax" on federal workers is only an accounting trick; this "tax" does not contribute to the government's income.

Let us take another step. Suppose we have a family of five; a mother, father and three sons. Suppose the mother and father both work and their combined income is $10,000 per month. Further assume each of the three boys gets $100 per month as an allowance. The boys use this money as petty cash, for video games, candy, etc.

Further assume that one day the father starts paying the boys in a different way. Suppose he writes each one a check for $100, but on the memo line he writes the following: $1000 minus $900 for household expenses = $100. Now the boys see the memo line and they start to assume that they also contribute to the household income. In fact they might claim, "We pay our share, too." After all, the father "deducted" $900 from each boy's check. The fact is, there was no deduction, it is only a trick in the paperwork, as the boys do not contribute to the household income. Notice that nothing has changed with the new method of payment; the boys are still getting their $100 each.

A good law would be to just pay all federal workers their current net pay without bothering with income tax. They ought to be exempt from paying taxes. The government would lose nothing, but all could then see the facts involved.

We need government to plan the economy.

For seventy-five years the communists in the Soviet Union planned everything in the economy. How many rolls of toilet paper to produce, how many televisions, where the factories ought to be, etc. All prices were fixed; all production was controlled. By the 1980s their economy collapsed. Conditions were horrendous; people were on a seven-year waiting list for a television. Government planning does not work because: *There is not enough planning.*

In a free economy, you will carefully plan the use of your money and property. You will do this on a daily basis, and you will understand your own needs better than anyone. In a free economy, everyone is a planner. In a dictatorship, bureaucrats do the planning and they cannot know all the intricacies involved.

Government can make us equal.

Many long to be equal. At least that is what they think. In truth, they don't long to be equal as much as they long to be free of envy.

No human will ever be equal to another. Even identical twins differ. If somehow a government managed to make all income equal, then other differences would arise, and the resentments would fester. If Mary Jones has the same income as everyone else, she will be faced with the resentment of her friend getting the more handsome husband or having longer legs or better hair. If everyone is handed an eight-ounce piece of fish, some pieces will have less bones than others, some will look fresher or have a better color.

When governments attempt to make all individual's *incomes* equal, the result is all individual's *output* becomes equal. This means that the smartest and hardest-working individuals in a free economy that earn higher incomes, will now lower their output under a system of forced equality. This loss of incentive by the smartest and best hurts the least able the most. Under this type of system, Eastern Europe rotted for 75 years.

You are not a bee in a hive or an ant on an anthill. Celebrate the fact that you are unique, you are different, and no one will ever be equal to you.

If you do not have control of your envy, then a government will never make you well. If you do not have control of your guilt for being successful, then don't advocate the enslavement of others to mitigate your illness. The guilt and envy is your fault and your weakness. Take control of your own mind.

16
The Fractional Reserve Banking System

The Federal Reserve System is the central banking system of the United States. It was established by law in 1913. The Federal Reserve is the regulator for America's fractional reserve banking system. It is called a "fractional reserve" system because banks are required to retain only a *fraction* of depositor's money in *reserve*. This fraction is currently 10%. For example, if you deposit $100 in an American bank, the bank is allowed to make loans of $90 with your money.

To simplify an example of the dangers involved, assume you are the bank's only customer and you deposit your $100. Now assume the bank loans $90 to Mr. Johnson. If, on the next day, you go to the bank to withdraw your $100, the bank will be in a state of insolvency, because it will only have $10 in its till. Of course, it never happens this way, because your bank has many depositors and many loans, and your bank is betting that not very many people will demand their money on any given day. To maintain a liquid position, the bank must accurately judge inflows of money from deposits and loan payments to withdrawals. This trick becomes a dangerous tightrope when the economy slows down, and thousands of fractional reserve banks have failed.[11]

As noted previously, intraspecies kleptoparasitism always involves deception. Fractional reserve banking is a very sophisticated deception. It is so clever a swindle that most people just cannot understand how it is harmful, let alone damaging, to their lives.

Imagine that you are a productive person and, referring to the example of your corn growing, you produce more corn than you need for your own consumption. In fact, the area where you live is very good corn-growing country and there are many corn farmers. You have plenty of corn left over and you barter much of this corn for the services of your local dentist, shoemaker and carpenter. After this bartering, you still have 1,000 bushels of corn left and decide to deposit this leftover corn in a local silo.

The man who owns this silo calls it the Corn Bank. It is made of steel and is waterproof. Your corn will be protected from the rain and snow and the steel walls cannot be compromised by vermin.

You pay him a 3% fee for the service, which amounts to 30 bushels of corn per year. He agrees to store your corn and tells you that you can get the corn at any time. You deposit your 1,000 bushels of corn with him. In turn, he gives you a deposit receipt and a checkbook. With each check you write, he charges a quarter bushel fee. This checkbook is very convenient for you in that you can now purchase things around your local village with these checks.

For example, if you need a few plumbing supplies for your farm; rather than taking several bushels of corn to your local plumbing supply store, you use the checks. You can write the check to the plumbing supply store in the following way: Pay to the bearer of this check 5 bushels of corn. The plumbing supply store has a good faith belief in this check because they know other merchants have been accepting these checks and they also know that, when the check is presented to the Corn Bank, the bank will turn over 5 bushels of corn to the bearer of the check.

Many other farmers in your area also deposit their corn in the Corn Bank. Corn Bank checks become a favorite currency in your area. A few people visit the Corn Bank every day, present the checks and take possession of their corn. Corn is now the new money. Understand that the paper checks are the *title* to the real money which is corn; they are not the money themselves. Like the title to your car, the paper title is only proof of ownership, it is not the actual car. Also realize that your car has a biological function; the paper title does not. At this point we can call the actual corn "money," and the paper checks, "currency."

The Corn Bank is doing a great business because it is so much easier for everyone to trade checks than the actual corn. After you write your check for the plumbing parts, the plumbing supply store can pick up the 5 bushels of corn from the Corn Bank, or they can use that piece of paper to purchase other things. For example, they could pay their employee with the same check. This check is good for 5 bushels of corn and the employee knows the check is good all over town. In time, almost everyone starts trading the paper corn checks rather than the corn itself.

A time comes when the Corn Bank offers checking accounts to everyone, and the operation of the Corn Bank has changed. To open an account, one does not need to deposit corn, but depositing currency has the same function: For every unit of currency there is a representative amount of actual money (corn) on deposit in the silo. Remember, these currency units, these checks, are a *promise* to deliver corn.

The plumbing supply store opens one of these accounts and deposits all the corn checks he receives. He can now write checks in any amount, say 15.25 bushels for example. Having the ability to write checks in small fractions of bushels makes things much easier and more precise. He prices things in his store accordingly: 10 bushels may become 9.99 bushels. After a time, he writes the amounts this way: B9.99.

Over time, the owner of the Corn Bank realizes that very few people will demand their corn on any one day. In fact, over a period of time only a small percentage of the corn inventory is actually removed. The banker then devises a plan after asking himself this question: "What if I were to make loans?"

His thought process works this way. "Suppose I make loans. I can do this by simply *adding* to the checking account balances of the borrowers. Not many people withdraw actual bushels of corn on any given month, so I can safely increase the paper receipts that represent the bushels of corn on deposit."

The banker now offers loans to people in your area. People become enthused and the economy booms with the new purchasing power.

How is it that there is now more purchasing power? The answer is that when the banker makes loans, the loans are actually *additional currency that has been loaned into existence.* For many, this is difficult to understand, but it works like this: When the banker makes a loan, he credits the checking account of the borrower for the amount of the loan. This increase in the checking account balances of the borrowers functions as additional purchasing power that did not exist previously. This additional currency, which is new purchasing power produced as a result of increased bank balances, now finds its way into the economy. When additional purchasing power enters an economy without a corresponding increase in the amount of goods, prices rise. This is often referred to as, "more money chasing fewer goods." This is the start of a classic "boom."

It is important to pause here and explain that these greater checking account balances do not increase the *money* supply, but rather increase the supply of the *claims* on money. Corn is the actual money and it has *biological attributes* and *biological value,* as we have seen. This biological value of the corn is *independent* of promises. However, these new claims on money (currency) *function* as money in the marketplace, but are *dependent* on promises, and, they *have no biological value.*

Suppose Mr. Smith borrows 500 bushels of corn form the corn bank. He does not get actual corn, but rather a checking account with B500 entered as the new balance. He also receives a book of checks. Mr. Smith then buys a new pair of shoes with a check written "pay the bearer on demand B24.99." Mr. Smith also buys a new chainsaw and washing machine. Many other people in your area get loans as well. The owner of the Corn Bank is now making a nice income from the interest he charges.

We should note here, that the increase in the amount of checking account balances brought about by the banker loaning money into existence is not really an increase in money, but an increase in currency. Corn is the actual money, the checks are only claims to that real money. In effect, the banker is secretly engaging in a fraud in that, *he is printing paper claims to products that do not exist.*

At this point, let us turn to an analogy. Suppose your neighbor had five identical 1932 Fords in storage. Moreover, suppose he printed 10 titles for each car and sold these titles to fifty different people, while offering free storage for their rare automobiles. Once in a while a holder of one of these titles will come in a take a car for a drive, but your neighbor never expects all of the title holders to show up at once. Do you see a problem here? Is your neighbor a truthful person? Can you trust him? Under current American law, *printing and selling titles for cars that do not exist is a fraud and a felony.*

With all of this new activity in the economy, the banker decides to open a branch of the corn bank that deals in currency only. This new bank does not have a silo, but it does have a silo motif. The walls are partially covered with galvanized metal corrugated paneling, the same sort of metal used on the walls of silos. The whole building looks strong. There are heavy brick walls with metal accents, and there is an impressive corn cob sculpture in the lobby. Hell, the thing is ten feet tall and gold plated.

The public is now sold on banking and the idea of using actual corn for trade seems to be falling to the wayside. This new bank offers free checking and new customers flock to this bank. As this bank receives currency deposits, it makes loans with most of this currency. For example, if 100 depositors deposit a total of B1000 in any month, the bank feels safe in making loans of B900. This new branch bank is now making a hefty profit by printing paper currency and charging interest for loaning paper claims (titles) to corn that does not exist.

Over a period of months you notice prices are heading higher. There are now many more Corn Bank checks in the marketplace driving up prices. The economy is buzzing with activity. The same plumbing parts that you bought last year for B5 are now B7. You now realize that your remaining balance of B700 in the Corn Bank is actually worth only about B500 in comparison to its former value in the market. You worked a very long time to achieve the good corn production levels you how have and were saving for a new tractor for your farm. A new tractor was B3,200, but now it is B4,500.

What is the *biological* significance of all of this? The significance is the fact that your stored labor, your biological energy, has been stolen by dilution. Your former purchasing power that was 1,000 bushels of corn has been reduced. The banker's deception has diluted your life's force.

Since you are learning to think like a "biologist of the most basic kind," you should place this in the context to the only thing that matters: *your biology.*

Fractional reserve banking is a form of intraspecies kleptoparasitism. It is an illness, and like a leach or other parasite, *it drains your biological energy.*

The antidote or cure for this disease is knowledge. If the general public had the knowledge of how the scam of fractional banking operates, the parasitic bankers could have never created this epidemic. Knowledge is your conceptual vaccine.

Notice that in your area, not only have prices risen, but people have begun behaving in strange ways. Prior to all the lending by the Corn Bank, people were modest and very careful with their spending. The shoemaker saved for years to buy a new sewing machine for his leathers, and the farmer next to you saved to improve his equipment every year. Homeowners saved wisely in order to slowly improve their homes and properties and most saved for their old age. Many saved for their children's education.

Gradually, with the introduction of all this new purchasing power, people are changing their habits. Many people in town buy swimming pools with their loans. The swimming pool contractor now has triple the business he did before. It is hard for him to get new labor, so he must raise the price he will pay his employees. He buys a new cement mixer that quadruples his output. He buys two new trucks and gets his wife several widgets for their new kitchen. Prices are now in an upward spiral. Businesses must now bid up the labor price. New businesses spring up.

If this boom lasts long enough, your son, who is now going to college, might change his career from soil science to swimming pool design. Your daughter might decide to be a fashion designer rather than a microbiologist.

The day will come when the new money runs out. The banker has loaned to his limit. The small amount of people that come to the Corn Bank to withdraw corn has now equaled the reserves of actual corn he holds in the silos. He attempts to get more deposits of corn by advertising free storage, free checking and a new toaster with every 100 bushels deposited. Some of the loans he made are not being paid back in full and on time. People seem to have all the swimming pools they want, and the people with newly acquired college degrees in swimming pool design can't get jobs. Many of these people paid for their college with loans from the Corn Bank. People slowly lose their enthusiasm and tighten their budgets. The swimming pool contractor is now building fewer swimming pools than before and is slow making his loan payments. He dismisses 20 employees, many of whom have taken loans from the Corn Bank to purchase big chrome wheels for their trucks or Grecian style gazebos for their backyards.

You notice that the whole culture of your community has changed since the Corn Bank started loaning excessive amounts of money. Prior to the fractional reserve inflation, people were very practical in that they saved for the future and the businesses saved for new equipment that would increase their production by improved efficiency. Many saved for an education that would bring them a life-long career. You suspect that this excessive lending has created a sort of disconnect from reality.

A rumor starts that the Corn Bank is in a little trouble. Many of the loans aren't being repaid and the cash flow at the bank declines. The paint on the silos at the Corn Bank is fading. The gold plating on the big corn cob sculpture is flaking off and sticking to the dirty carpet. The bank dismisses a few employees. You get a little suspicious and decide to withdraw your corn and store it at your own small wooden silo, not as safe from vermin or theft, but you have a suspicious feeling about it all. The Corn Bank owner is indignant. He senses you have lost faith in the Corn Bank and he assures you that all is well. He attempts to talk you out of withdrawing your corn, but you insist. You don't know at the time that there are paper checks from the Corn Bank totaling a million bushels of corn but the silos contain only 10% of that amount. Rumors start and a few other depositors remove their corn. Soon there is a long line at the Corn Bank, but the corn is not there. The Corn Bank must now close its doors.

The swimming pool contractor closes his doors and stops making payments on all his loans. The young people with college degrees in swimming pool design, aroma therapy, music appreciation, art history, and fashion design look for work and demand justice. The economy contracts. The Corn Bank must now foreclose on many of its borrowers. The Corn Bank's attorneys place liens on the properties that have loans that bought swimming pools, gazebos, kitchen remodeling and saunas. Lawsuits abound.

During the legal battles it is found that the Corn Bank is a corporation and the owner and founder is legally just another employee. He is shocked that all of this could happen. His large salary and big bonuses over the years have provided him with plenty of purchasing power. He retires to his home at the country club and plays golf seven days per week. In the winter, he stays at his residence in Hawaii.

If you haven't borrowed money for senseless widgets, you might be sheltered. You still have your cornfield. You have the knowledge of how to grow corn. People will always need to eat, but they will not always need to swim. Your children move back in with you. You notice they are demoralized and no longer have practical values. Your son can't seem to get the idea of how to hold a shovel and spends much of his time playing on the video machine he bought with borrowed money from the Corn Bank. Your daughter daydreams about fashion.

This thought experiment is only a small and very incomplete model of how fractional banking works. In today's world, the complexity is much greater. However, we are not attempting to fully explain the interworkings of fractional reserve banking, but only outline some principles involved.

Fractional reserve banking achieves three things. First, it steals biological energy from its victims; second, it causes irrational investments to emerge; and third, if this style of banking lasts for a couple of decades before a crash cleans out the system, a whole generation will be mislead about the nature of rational living.

When the economy rebuilds by cleaning out all the irrational investments and bad loans, the economy will need welders, programmers, mechanics, agronomists, chemists, engineers, etc. What will be available are fashion designers, psychologists, sociologists, gazebo consultants and palm readers.

Today, fractional reserve banking is promoted and controlled by governments. The beneficiaries of all this stolen biological energy are the bankers, financiers and others who get in on the ground floor and exit with their loot before the crash. We can rightfully label these bankers as klepto-parasites. They engaged in a fraud that ought to be a felony. However, the government sponsors this fraud by making it legal. Is it possible that the politicians have their hands in the banker's pockets?

America has been in a fraction reserve boom for several decades, with only intermittent slowdowns that have never fully corrected the irrationality by a total cleanout of the system. It is important to understand that governments create fractional reserve booms by the lowering of reserve requirements of banks and the setting of low interest rates. The current boom was intensified by government policies of pushing the banks to lower the lending requirements for home ownership. A great portion of the American economy was driven into the housing boom and directed away from more sensible investments. Large, five-bedroom homes were sold to low-income workers who had no chance of supporting the debt loads. More money was pushed into student loans. Millions of people who should have been welders, mechanics, equipment operators, garbage men and the like borrowed billions to obtain degrees in worthless subjects.

When the system fails *due to faulty government regulations and the government sponsorship of fraud*, the politicians rant about the faulty system, they blame the "unregulated free market," and then use these lies as a justification to create more government controls and power.

17
Envy

You have an envious voice, a very small but powerful voice in the deep recesses of your mind. This voice silently speaks to you when you see the success of others. This voice depends on your willingness to suspend rationality. You have probably never thought about this voice, but it is there. It is very sneaky. It lingers in your subconscious and causes pain. Oftentimes, this pain will remain anonymous and you may never know its source.

This voice can be controlled. You can easily make this voice your friend and use it to enhance rather than degrade your life.

Let's try a thought experiment. Suppose you lived in England a few hundred years ago. Further assume you grew up in a village near the king's castle. At a very young age, you worked on the family farm. You spent much of the year working the fields with your parents.

Your neighbor, let us call him John, lives close by and you two are childhood friends. Like you, he works the fields with his parents. One day John meets a servant of the king and is taken to the king's castle. He gets a job working for the king. In just a few weeks, you see him everywhere in his new uniform. This uniform is crisp and clean, adorned with crests and symbols, and he looks very official. This is when your envious voice creeps into your subconscious and you begin to experience the pangs of envy. John's success will eat away at you and you will feel pain. His gains are now your pains.

Let us now move to the present day. You work as an assistant manager at a local store. Your childhood friend, let us call him Steve, works at another store as an assistant manager. He is also your neighbor and owns a home next to yours. One day he gets a promotion. He is now store manager and gets a big raise in pay. Over a period of a few weeks, you see a new sports car in his driveway. When he invites you and a few others over to watch a football game, you learn that he has a new television — a gigantic screen — and you see other things about the house that you could have only dreamt of.

This is where the voice of envy silently speaks to you. You feel that resentment. Even though you do not understand it openly, you are comparing yourself with Steve. Suddenly, you begin to dislike Steve. You may not know why you dislike him, but the resentment slowly creeps in.

"This is where you could have been," your subconscious telegraphs to your envy center. The problem is, your envious voice uses a secret code. It never telegraphs the actual words to your consciousness, only the negative results. Your envious voice never sends reasoned arguments; it only sends the feelings we call resentment.

Steve is now the source of your emotional pain. Steve causes you pain, therefore Steve is bad. This is the most important point. *Steve causes you pain, therefore Steve is bad*. Your envy boils it all down ever further: *Steve is bad*. You are now primed for the propaganda of the politicians: "*The rich are evil, inequality is evil…*"

Now, let us analyze the real situation. When you lived in England a few hundred years ago, you were living without electrical power. You worked daylight till dark pulling weeds on your family's farm. You had no central heating, no hot water, no plumbing. To get a drink of water in the winter, you had to break through the ice layer in your wooden bucket. You did not have modern medicine. Your teeth rotted out by the age of 30. Your life expectancy was only 40.

It is easy to understand that you can have these envy pains regardless of the facts involved. Notice that today, while you are assistant manager in your local store, you live far better than the King of England did 300 years ago. Your life expectancy is almost double the king's. You can walk into a dark room, flip a switch and get light. You are warm in your house. You have several changes of clothes, whereas in England 300 years ago you had very few. Today, your local market is stuffed with fresh produce, canned goods, fresh meat and foods from all over the world.

This goes to show that envy is not objective or reasonable; it is only relative. Make no mistake: The man who has a billion dollars and a sixty-foot yacht will envy the man who has five billion dollars and a hundred-foot yacht.

Your envy is a natural emotion and doesn't always cause damage. For example, you could view your neighbor who is now a store manager in two or more ways. Your emotion of envy might propel you to work harder on your job to achieve a promotion. You might decide to change jobs. Or, you might ask your neighbor for advice on how to do better.

Another avenue is to fall into a mental state of resentment. You could abandon your reason and blame your perceived lack of success on "the system." You are now fully primed and ready to receive the propaganda of the politicians. You fall for all of it. "The system is unfair," you think, "people like Steve ought to be taxed more." Your envious voice secretly thinks, "They ought to strip away some of his success and bring him down to my level."

Envy can be a highly irrational emotion because it will and *has* led to the destruction of whole societies. Envy can be propagated by propaganda and fueled to such intensity that *you would rather see your neighbor destroyed by government than have your freedom to your own life*. This is the insanity of the envious voice.

Envy can also lead to a general decline in productivity. If you live in a highly envious culture, you might choose to hide your success. Rather than have your neighbors resent your achievements, give you the evil eye and hate you like you hate Steve, you might choose to work less and achieve less. You will have a motivation to achieve less in life if your achievements are frowned upon.

The best way to deal with your envious voice is to recognize it and embrace it. Rather than wishing harm to your neighbor, Steve, enjoy the fact that he is not envying you, and you are actually in a safer position than he is. If you want a new sports car like his, get a second job or get training that teaches you how to be a better employee. Use your neighbor's success as a template for your own life. Surrendering to the destructive side and negative consequences of your envious voice will never enhance your life.

Many upper middle class Americans who advocate income equality via wealth redistribution are covertly seeking to diminish the shine of those more successful than themselves. Their secret goal, realized or unconscious, is one that strives more for the debasing of the highly successful than the elevation of the poor. They are the closet enviers. They own *large* homes, and yet, they envy those who own *gigantic* homes. They pine for the social status of those above themselves and look to government to level the playing field. They seek relief from the nagging problem that is their undefined pain of envy. The shine of those above them is just too bright. This advocacy for more government predation on the wealthy is always masked by their feigned empathy for the poor. The fact that those in "poverty" in a modern capitalist society live better than the kings of ancient history makes little difference. The poor will *never* have enough in their view and there will *never* be enough government predation. *The secret psychology of income redistribution is to bring down those above, not help those below.*

Those who project their envy into the social structure and claim to seek "justice" through government-enforced income equality are doing nothing more than kicking the can of resentment down the road. Regardless of their achievements in changing the system, regardless of how much redistribution is achieved, this resentment will never leave their minds.

The can will never be out of their sight, because no two people will ever be exactly the same. More and more government power will be demanded with disastrous results.

The management of envy can only be controlled by the individual mind. With practice and understanding, you can control and change your envy from the negative to the positive. It is not someone else's responsibility, and they couldn't do it for you anyway. If you want to control your envy, it is *your* job.

In one aspect, government is a protection racket. Many give up their freedoms in the marketplace in exchange for envy appeasement, and the rich receive guilt placation.

You want to be independent, free and have self-worth. You want to feel good about the direction of your life. You will never have these good feelings if you are envious. If you are worried about what others have done, you have less passion for living by your own vision. A person with self-esteem is a person who is the master of his envy.

18
Environmentalism

As we have discussed, human intraspecies parasitism requires deception. The victims are usually deceived in such a way as to assist the predators in carrying out their plans.

For decades, and you will remember this if you were born prior to 1950, the Soviet Union flooded the world with propaganda that claimed the Soviet Union out- produced the United States and other western countries. The claim was that their agricultural production, steel production, basic manufacturing and economic well-being was far superior to the rest of the non-socialist world. Moreover, they boasted that Marxism, that is, state ownership of the means of production, was the new guiding light. Despite their locked-down slave society, bits of factual information leaked out. By the 1960s, this leakage of truth was a developing problem for the communists. At this point the American Left went to work to prepare a substitute propaganda.

The Soviet Union collapsed and by 1990 the real story was laid bare for all to see. The Soviets were in complete poverty and had been so for the entire time communism was in control. All the stories about superior production and the good life that communism brings were lies. There were famines; millions of people starved to death. Their seventy-year claim that the communist system produced more and better goods was a complete fabrication.

The Left needed a new propaganda. The new propaganda was the following:

Capitalism and human freedom does out-produce socialism or communism, but production itself is really the problem. Why? Because it requires that humans change the environment, and any change to the environment disrupts nature.

To state it another way: *We can't win the propaganda war by lying about how much better production is under a socialist rule, so let's lie and claim that human production itself will destroy the Earth.*

The great majority of people are extremely ignorant and gullible. This fact is easily demonstrated by the most casual look at history. That millions of Germans could believe in Hitler's rants, that millions of Russians could worship Stalin and that even more millions of Chinese could believe Mao Zedong, prove the point. And of course, there is much more. Billions of humans believe in voodoo, unicorns, witchcraft and other delusional ideas. It is no surprise that they swallow the biggest delusional idea of them all: Environmentalism.

Two hundred million years ago, dinosaurs roamed the Earth and dined on plant species that are extinct today. Things change. Continents shift, the sun's output varies, the Earth's orbit and its corresponding distance from the sun changes in long cycles lasting thousands of years. New species of pathogens come into existence and devastate nonresistant species. Tides change over the millenniums due to the fact that the moon is slowly moving farther away from the Earth. From time to time, large meteors strike the Earth with disastrous consequences.

Mass extinctions occur. Volcanic activity can peak and bury tens of thousands of square miles in lava. Explosive volcanoes can cover continent-sized areas in suffocating ash that will wipe out entire ecosystems. Fine volcanic ash can be suspended in the atmosphere for months or even years causing large shifts in climate.

These shifts can cause the complete extinction or relocation of species. The Earth can undergo dramatic changes in climate due to events that took place millions of years ago and many trillions of miles from Earth. A supernova, an exploding star several million light years from Earth, can send cosmic rays that can enhance cloud formation. These clouds reflect light and can cool the Earth's climate for years.[12]

These same cosmic rays can strike the DNA in any species of life and cause a mutation that can change a harmless bacterium into a deadly disease that can wipe out a species. The Earth is not a static place that, if it were not for man, would remain unchanged. The Earth has been in a constant flux for billions of years, and long before any human came into existence.

The idea that change is unfavorable is delusional. If the Earth had not radically changed from its early state about five billion years ago, there would be no whales, butterflies or humans.

Another thought experiment: Suppose you are a cyanobacterium. You are just one of trillions of them living about three billion years ago on Earth. Further assume you can think and form ideas much like you can today. From your viewpoint, the Earth is a very old place; it is your Mother Earth, about two billion years old. Two thousand million years old — wow, what a grand place! *Let's not change it*, you think.

At that time, the Earth had little oxygen in the atmosphere. You lived with your trillions of friends and family and were basically slime in wet environments, or otherwise just drifted along in the oceans. You and your friends were very hard at work and were involved in the heavy production of oxygen and did something amazing in those years: You completely changed the environment and killed off trillions of anaerobic organisms. In fact, using the reasoning methods of the present day environmentalists, *your species destroyed Mother Earth.*

At this point, millions of your friends start a movement that claims cyanobacteria are evil in that your actions are killing Mother Earth and changing the environment. *They claim that the creation of oxygen is not natural.* In fact, little will you know that in the future, a species named *homo sapiens* will also change the environment, but this change will pale in comparison to what you are doing. You and your species are radically destroying your environment. Despite all the warnings, you continue and over millions of years, you radically change the Earth's atmosphere.

In time, oxygen levels become so elevated that oxygen-tolerant and oxygen-loving species of life now dominate the Earth. Many of those species of life that were intolerant of oxygen have been killed off. They are extinct or have gone underground. You and your kind are responsible for the mass extinction of many native species. Native species! Trillions upon trillions are dead. You and all of your cyanobacteria friends and family are responsible. Should you start a movement to limit population growth?

Just as cyanobacteria are natural to this planet, you are natural to this planet. It is your nature to change the environment. Over billions of years, many species and various geological forces have made drastic changes to the Earth. For example, broad leaf trees (angiosperms) have choked out vast areas of conifers (gymnosperms).

About 65 million years ago, in an area is known as the Deccan Traps, a volcanic eruption of basalt flooded India with 200,000 square miles of lava with a thickness of about one mile. This eruption lasted for about 25,000 years and drastically changed the Earth's climate and contributed to the demise of thousands, if not millions, of species. Millions upon millions of tons of toxic volcanic gases were released into the atmosphere. This event, along with the Chicxulub impact event, is considered by many to be the source of a great mass extinction known as the Cretaceous–Paleogene extinction.

The Earth is not static and unchanging. In a process known as plate tectonics, whole continents are pulled apart and then are pushed under other continents. Ice ages occur every few thousand years and kill trillions of trees, mammals, reptiles and insects. Continents collide and create mountain ranges where oceans previously existed. These oceans dry up and species become extinct. Earthquakes create tsunamis and these massive waves can inundate large areas and kill millions of plants and animals.

To believe that humans have a large impact on the planet is delusional. Quoting Dr. George Reisman:

> "...the total of the supply of minerals mined by man each year amounts to substantially less than 25 cubic miles. This is a rate that could be sustained for the next 100 million years before it amounted to something approaching 1 percent of the supply represented by the earth... Mining operations could be carried on at 100 times their present scale for a million years and still claim less than 1 percent of the earth." [13]

Another delusion is that the Earth is overpopulated and that humans are taking over all available space. To place this delusion in perspective: If the entire state of California held the same population density as the principality of Monaco - California alone would house the entire Earth's population of seven billion humans, with over 10,000 square miles to spare. California is but 1/1000 of the area of the Earth, that is, one tenth of one percent. To supply the Earth's population with food, the farming area necessary to feed this population would be about 1.4 acres per person, the land now farmed per person in the United States.[14] This is a very generous amount of land and not only accounts for food for humans, but also food grown for farm animals and export. Assuming 1.4 acres per person for farming, this equals 9.8 billion acres of farmland needed to feed the world on a very generous American diet. Since the Earth's area is 196,939,900 sq. miles, with 30% being land, there is approximately 59,081,970 sq. miles of land on Earth. A square mile of land equals 640 acres of land. The land portion of Earth is therefore 59,081,970 X 640 = 37,812,460,800 or 37.8 billion acres.

If it takes 9.8 billion acres of farm land to feed 7 billion humans, this amounts to approximately 26% of the Earth's land, and represents about 8% of the entire surface of the Earth. Of course, humans fish, but fishing in the ocean is a transitory activity and is not occupation. If we were to add this area that fishing boats occupy at any one time, the number would be trivial.

Consider this:

"There are about 2,200 described species of earthworms in the world. They vary from small kinds, such as the one-inch tree worms that live under rotting wood and bark, to the gigantic kinds found in tropical countries — some of them seven or more feet long when fully stretched out. Some are pallid in color; some are red-brown or purple; a few are gaily colored, such as the green-worm of Europe and North America, and a Philippine species that is mottled with bright blue. Most of them prefer alkaline soils but a few will live in acid soils and we know of two species that live in decomposing manure. Some kinds live in the wet mud of riverbanks; two or three thrive in the filter beds of sewage treatment plants, and there are a few that actually have gills and are entirely aquatic.

.....In very favorable conditions, there may be an many as two million earthworms per acre, but none in very sandy soils. Darwin estimated that 50,000 worms per acre may carry more than 18 tons of soil to the surface in a single year."[15]

Consider the following. A small earthworm weighs about 3 grams. If we use the above numbers of between 50,000 and 2,000,000 earthworms per acre[19], we can safely assume one million per acre. However, to make sure we are not overdoing it, let's cut that number down by 75% and use the figure of 250,000. Since few earthworms live in sandy soils, and we can assume few live in the arctic regions, we can discard 75% of the Earth's landmass as being unfavorable to earthworms. This leaves us with 9 billion acres of earthworms, with each acre holding 250,000. With 250,000 earthworms per acre, and each weighing 3 grams, we see that the average weight per acre of earthworms is 250,000 X 3 grams = 750,000 grams which is 750 kilograms. A kilogram = 2.2 pounds. This gives us 1,650 pounds of earthworms per acre. Assuming 9 billion acres of land that is favorable to earthworm development, we have 9,000,000,000 x 1650 = 14,850,000,000,000. This is 14.8 trillion pounds of earthworms in the ground on planet Earth. How much do humans weigh? With 7 billion humans at an average weight of 105 pounds, we get a number of 7,000,000,000 X 105 = 735,000,000,000; this is 735 billion pounds of humans on Earth. Using these numbers, *the mass of earthworms is about 20 times greater than that of humans.* I encourage you to do some research yourself.

This same principle can be applied to many different life forms. For example, it has been shown that termites produce far more methane than human activity, about 20 million tons per year.[16]

Are ants taking over the planet? In an article by NPR, the estimate is that ants outweigh humans by nine-fold.[17] Humans weight about 47 million tons, whereas ants weigh about 423 million tons. Other estimates take the ratio of ants to humans as far as 30X.

We automatically assume that humans are taking over the planet simply because many of us live in cities and travel on roads. We tend to stay in areas were other humans are active. We watch television and see humans, we read magazines and see humans. Newspapers are mostly about human news. Combine these facts with the daily hemorrhaging of environmentalist propaganda, and it is quite natural for you to believe that humans are over-running the planet.

Humans have little impact on the planet, but the propaganda from the Left hammers out the idea that humans are destroying everything. Children are taken prisoner for several hours per day, forced into government schools and brainwashed with this propaganda from a very early age.

It would take several thousand pages to thoroughly refute the environmentalist propaganda, and even then, they will change their methods and embark on another course of lies. It is a thousand times easier to tell a lie than to refute a lie. Imagine this: Your neighbor tells you that your favorite tree is dying from a strange disease. You immediately hire a plant pathologist to investigate. Your neighbor's lie was easy; it only took him five seconds to tell it. However, your investigation took several thousand dollars and several weeks of expensive research to refute his simple lie.

When the television news says the following or something similar — "Scientists say that fossil fuels are making the Earth warmer" — notice that they seldom give the names of the scientists, and notice it would take a massive amount of money and time to refute their claims. (Something the television news will never tell you: 30,000 scientists, 9,000 of which are PhDs, have signed a petition stating human caused global warming is not proven science.)[18]

Governments are entrenched with statists who wish to take what freedoms you have remaining. Universities are also entrenched. Billions of dollars are spent yearly on scientific studies carried out by university scientists who are seeking government grant money. This grant money naturally flows to those scientists who walk and talk the government line of deception. Few government bureaucrats will knowingly fund research that shows governments lie, enslave, murder and use fake science to do so. The great majority of news journalists attended government schools and universities. They enter their field with a statist mindset. They slant and manipulate the news to fit their hopes of a utopian society based on intraspecies predation.

Another phony science, eugenics, held the attention of the world for decades during the late nineteenth and early twentieth centuries. Universities were entrenched with the science. Prominent world leaders and scientists were fooled.

Quoting Edwin Black:

> "Eugenics was the racist pseudoscience determined to wipe away all human beings deemed "unfit," preserving only those who conformed to a Nordic stereotype. Elements of the philosophy were enshrined as national

policy by forced sterilization and segregation laws, as well as marriage restrictions, enacted in twenty-seven states. In 1909, California became the third state to adopt such laws. Ultimately, eugenics practitioners coercively sterilized some 60,000 Americans, barred the marriage of thousands, forcibly segregated thousands in "colonies," and persecuted untold numbers in ways we are just learning. Before World War II, nearly half of coercive sterilizations were done in California, and even after the war, the state accounted for a third of all such surgeries....

"Eugenics would have been so much bizarre parlor talk had it not been for extensive financing by corporate philanthropies, specifically the Carnegie Institution, the Rockefeller Foundation and the Harriman railroad fortune. They were all in league with some of America's most respected scientists hailing from such prestigious universities as Stanford, Yale, Harvard and Princeton. These academicians espoused race theory and race science, and *then faked and twisted data* to serve eugenics' racist aims. (Italics from Hugh)

"Stanford president David Starr Jordan originated the notion of "race and blood" in his 1902 racial epistle *Blood of a Nation*, in which the university scholar declared that human qualities and conditions such as talent and poverty were passed through the blood."[19]

From Wikipedia:

"The methods of implementing eugenics varied by country; however, some of the early 20th century methods involved identifying and classifying individuals and their families, including the poor, mentally ill, blind, deaf,

developmentally disabled, promiscuous women, homo-
sexuals, and racial groups (such as the Roma and Jews in
Nazi Germany) as "degenerate" or "unfit", the segregation
or institutionalization of such individuals and groups, their
sterilization, euthanasia, and their mass murder. The practice of euthanasia was carried out on hospital patients in
the Aktion T4 centers such as Hartheim Castle. Eugenics
became an academic discipline at many colleges and universities, and received funding from many sources. Three
International Eugenics Conferences presented a global
venue for eugenists with meetings in 1912 in London, and
in 1921 and 1932 in New York. Eugenic policies were first
implemented in the early 1900s in the United States. Later,
in the 1920s and 30s, the eugenic policy of sterilizing cer-
tain mental patients was implemented in other countries,
including Belgium, Brazil, Canada, and Sweden. The scientific reputation of eugenics started to decline in the 1930s,
a time when Ernst Rüdin used eugenics as a justification
for the racial policies of Nazi Germany."[20]

Eugenics was the dominant pseudo-scientific mass delusion 100 years
ago. Millions were murdered as a result. Hitler used eugenics to underpin
his racial policies that killed millions of Jews. In his view, it was necessary
to rid Germany, and eventually the world, of this inferior race.

With environmentalism, all humans are inferior, with the exception
of the environmentalists themselves. Environmentalists have continually
hinted at the need for population control. Quoting Prince Phillip, (husband of The Queen of England) Duke of Edinburgh: "In the event that
I am reincarnated, I would like to return as a deadly virus, to contribute
something to solving overpopulation."[21]

The wish to destroy humans is ingrained in environmentalism. Billions
have accepted the idea that humans are not natural to Earth, and billions more hold to the idea that man is naturally burdened and tainted by

original sin. When these two delusions are combined, the possibilities are horrific. If eugenics was responsible for the deaths of millions by gassing, imagine the consequences in a world of nuclear weapons.

The real underlying goal of the environmentalist movement, a goal that even the great majority of environmentalists do not understand, is:

Environmentalism is designed to obstruct and obliterate the naturally occurring drive for humans to own and direct the use of property.

Without a connection to property, you will feel an impotence towards the world. You will feel obligated toward a "hands off" approach to reality. You will be isolated from your nature. Your nature is to manipulate the materials of nature, to create, to engage the physical world. Environmentalism tricks you into believing your nature is evil, in that, everything you do to act on physical reality is wrong, that is, if it does not conform to their rules. Of course, their rules will continually change, until you are completely powerless.

According to the environmentalists, everything you own has an impact on the environment. You cannot discard a piece of paper, fertilize your lawn, grow your own food, drive your car, flush your toilet, or heat your house without some law or government mandate to pigeonhole you into submission. It will get worse, until your every action will be directed by government.

Property is the foundation of human freedom. To understand that thousands, if not millions, of life forms have a self-defense and property mandate directed by the encoding in their DNA molecule is of the highest importance. The environmentalists want to destroy human freedom, and the destruction of the idea of property is their path.

You only own something when you can direct its use. If the government tells you how to mow your lawn, you do not own your lawn. You are nothing more than a caretaker of the lawn that is owned by the government. With the pretense of protecting the environment, governments are seizing control of everything you own. Ownership implies control. If you can't direct and control your property's use, then "ownership" is just another hoax perpetuated by the intraspecies parasites.

There is a final and extremely important thought you ought to consider about environmentalism. Ask yourself this question: "What is the environment?" The dictionary will tell you it is "surrounding things" as one meaning. Another meaning will be "nature." Merriam Webster Dictionary defines it as "the conditions that surround someone or something: the conditions and influences that affect the growth, health, progress, etc., of someone or something."

The Oxford Dictionary gives us several definitions; one of them is, "the natural world, as a whole or in a particular geographical area, especially as affected by human activity."

Environment is a nebulous word, is it not? It *is* vague to most people. They assume it is important. We hear it every day. Well, what is it?

An exact answer to this question exposes the hidden secret of the environmentalist's evil intent. Think this through very carefully, as this is the definition they want you to *feel* but not fully understand:

The environment is everything on the planet Earth with the exception of humans and the products humans create.

Thinking this through carefully will possibly lead you to the conclusion that the actual objective of the environmentalists is to erase human nature.

When an environmentalist says, *"We must protect the environment,"* he is really saying, *"We must suppress human nature."* Your nature requires you, or someone working on your behalf, to make changes to naturally occurring things and convert them to products you need to maintain and extend your life. You *must* cut down a tree to get lumber. You *must* destroy trees, brush and clear land so that you can grow food. You *must* dig a hole in the ground to get iron ore. You *must* build a fire to smelt this ore. You *must* kill an animal and eat it.

At the core of environmentalism is misanthropy, the hatred of human beings. The source of this hatred can only be imagined.

One source that is highly suspect is Christianity. God created a perfect world with perfect creatures and a perfect Garden of Eden. And then, *by the catastrophic and sinful action of eating a fruit*, Man wrecks the utopia. Man's evil nature is suddenly a blight to the otherwise impeccable order of things. Man is the *exception* to an idyllic world, he is *unnatural*, he is an outcast. It is not difficult to imagine that this widely accepted myth is the likely foundation of the psychological uneasiness experienced when a Christian hears any refutation of environmentalism. They have accepted as fact the evilness of all humans. If humans are evil in the eyes of God because they wrecked a perfect Garden of Eden, it seems quite likely that these same evil humans are currently destroying an otherwise perfect Earth. In fact, a Christian could easily come to the conclusion that it was all predictable.

The hatred for those who are successful is another possibility. Somewhere in their youth, the environmentalists may have encountered minds far superior to their own, and the bitterness of envy grew into a labyrinth of resentment that even they cannot comprehend. They resent success, and the underlying and hidden intent of the environmentalist movement is the total control of humans, especially *successful* humans, by forbidding the expression of the naturally occurring human biology that requires self-ownership and ownership of property. Environmentalists, like all Leftists, cannot tolerate those who are independent and shine too brightly.

19
What you can do

No dictatorship can succeed with a populace free of delusion.

Obviously, the first action you ought to take is that of freeing yourself from delusions. Many of the important ones are outlined in this book. The most important delusions to conquer: *duty, rights, original sin* and the *unnaturalness of man*.

Many economic myths can be resolved by a study of the free market. See the books listed in the recommended reading section.

Another delusion that can hinder your life is the belief that the stray data that is a product of your incredibly powerful brain has some deeper meaning. If you don't exercise control over your vague thoughts, you will lose the reigns on your reasoning, your rational mind. You will be subject to a multitude of mental scams. You might come to believe that crystals will lead you into a more meaningful world, that a psychic can read your future, or that you have fallen victim to a curse. Take control of yourself. Your brain is the most powerful machine in the known universe, get control of it, and learn how to logically hammer on every idea the intraspecies predators offer.

All dictatorships use delusion like a slight-of-hand trick to lull the people into self-doubt, guilt and envy. The rich are made to feel guilt, those with less are made to feel envy, and all are driven towards alienation of the self from the nature of human biology. The politicians who are intraspecies parasites depend on your vague thoughts and unfocused mind to give credence to their ideas.

The Egyptian pharaohs held the people's minds by the awe of the gold ornaments and gigantic pyramids. They ruled under the auspices of the "divine rights of kings." This symbolism held power over the people. Symbolism is void of fact, but ripe with emotion. These emotion-fueled delusions held by the Egyptian populace contributed to their own enslavement.

You most likely believe that you must recycle to save the world. You probably believe that public education is a must, otherwise all children would be illiterate. You might get a thrill when you see an engraved eagle on a shiny brass government plaque. You are fully impressed by the gallantry of the American military as it carries the waving flag known as Old Glory across the planet. If you are a woman, you might even get sexually aroused when you see your favorite politician. Thousands of women fainted in the presence of Adolf Hitler. Hitler was known to the German people as the "High Protector of the Holy Mountain," an empty concept void of all but emotional meaning, and it fooled millions, many of whom were accomplished scientists and scholars.

Despots the world over fool the people with their claims of being close to God or having a divine message. They wear their military medals by the dozen. If they do not display grandiose adornments, they speak in a grandiose language that points to some sort of utopia. When held up to the light of reason, these speeches usually mean little, but the speakers know how to pull the emotional strings that are attached to the underlying delusions.

If you cling to these delusions and are impressed by any politician, you need to take a cold conceptual shower and rethink your ideas. The majority of politicians are likely psychopaths. Few politicians want to reduce government power. They argue with each other about how to apply power, but rarely do they try to reduce it. A healthy way to think is to assume all of them are enemies to your life until proven otherwise.

America was founded on the premise of natural rights. We have seen that this premise is not valid. The Founding Fathers were correct in the direction they took. Their natural rights concept was false, but they did the very best they could. They correctly sensed that human self-ownership is the underlying nature of man; they just did not have a rational way to describe it.

America has something very important woven in the structure of its law: private property. This fabric has been worn very thin over the past two hundred years, but it is the only political concept that matters. *All freedom comes from the property concept, and property is a biological attribute, a scientific fact.*

All meaningful legal rights stem from property rights. The legal right to a free press means you can write on your own paper, that is, paper that is *your* property. You cannot write on your neighbor's walls. Your neighbor's property trumps your legal right to the freedom of the press.

(Notice that legal rights and natural rights are totally different concepts, in that, the theory of *natural rights* implies an attribute of human nature, whereas *legal rights* are a human legal construct designed to regulate action.)

The legal right to speak your mind is a property right. Your larynx is your property. However, you do not have the legal right to seize your neighbor's microphone to give a speech, as the microphone is your *neighbor's* property.

If you have the legal right to your property, then there can be no dictatorship. Your own property starts with your mind and body and extends to those things created by you and gained by you in trade with others. As long as a government abstains from any controls or parasitism on your property, you are free politically.

To change America and get it back on a track towards freedom, all that is needed is a strong advocacy for property rights. If you get involved with politics, then property is the only thing that matters.

This property includes money. Money is a naturally occurring entity that arises from peaceful trade between individuals. Money is not a creation of government, but rather, its meaning has been *seized* by governments. To advocate freedom, you must advocate the severance of money from government. When a government places its name on money, it is claiming ownership of money's roots. This claim is given credibility by the ignorance of the real meaning of money and is enforced by the psychology of authority. *When a government puts its name on your money, it is putting its name on your biology.*

One problem that many people must face while contemplating life in a free society is fear. This fear comes from the realization that they will no longer be an intraspecies parasite. Like a long term criminal being released from prison, they will gain freedom, but they fear that they will no longer be housed, fed and told what to do.

The fear of no longer being a parasite is quite likely the backbone for the failure to roll back the gains in the welfare state. Even self-reliant people are apprehensive when they face the prospect of not having a "safety net" of government-guaranteed income and services.

"I will need people to take care of me when I'm old," is just another way of saying, "I will need the government to help me be a parasite on others."

When you vote for a politician that promises to assist you in being a parasite, you are actually a co-conspirator in kleptoparasitism. Remember, kleptoparasitism requires delusion, trickery and violence. This is a worthy thought to consider. Another thought is that millions of species employ self-defense measures to guard against parasitism. Ask yourself what will happen to your government safety net when enough people wake up to these facts and start defending themselves? Will you have a safety net then?

A delusion that still stands, even after countless refutations, is the delusion that, without government safety nets, people will live in abject poverty in their old age, and even the young and able will falter and suffer. This delusion is rubbish and one of the grand tricks the predators of the world have used through out history to gain power. You need government, they claim, a government that will protect you from foreign enemies, terrorism, greedy businessmen, and the poverty of old age. The propaganda is massive and permeates the culture. A few insightful people have written books disproving the propaganda, but those who wish to quash your sovereignty have won the information and propaganda war.

The most rational course you can take is to begin the mental process of weaning yourself away from being one of these parasites. If you work for the government, tell yourself the truth: You are working for an oppressive organization, and you are a parasite yourself. Take steps to learn a new career in the private sector. Take the sanction property pledge. Start saving for your future. Once you start down this road, it will become easier with each day.

Self-education is the most important thing you can do. Read some of the books from the recommended reading list. You will find that government control hampers the economy to a great extent. The reason you now need government assistance is because the government has not only hampered the economy, it has siphoned off a great deal of your wealth, money you could have saved for your future. The evidence of this is available in many books and on the internet.

If you do work for the government and *honestly* can't find a way out, then refuse to engage in violence on the government's behalf. If the Nazi war criminals had refused to engage in mass murder, the world could have been a different place. They could have feigned incompetence on their jobs. Many of them could have found a way to resist assisting the government-ordered brutality and murder.

Understand your envy. If you get a sickening feeling when your neighbor gets a new car or wins the lottery, learn to identify this feeling. This emotion can hamper your enjoyment of life. It can also propel you into taking actions that are detrimental to your financial welfare. For example, you might feel pressured into buying an expensive new car to impress your friends and neighbors. These feelings are most likely unconscious and therefore unrealized. Your envy can control so many of your decisions that you may buy this fancy car just to *avoid* feeling envy.

Free yourself from your major delusions. Look for the signs of your delusions by applying the scientific idea of finding measurements. If something can't be measured, it may not be a valid concept.

Once you begin to think in terms of biology, you will learn that you are a super intelligent, property owning, self-defending, and sometimes delusional animal. You will begin to see through the foggy veil that is the façade of the government. You will think in terms of fundamentals. Your mind will hone itself into a sharp instrument that can dissect untruths and cut through the haze that is pumped out from behind the great façade.

A likeness of this façade was depicted in the movie, *The Wizard of Oz*. A much more detailed depiction of this façade can be found in George Orwell's monumental novel, *1984*.

The external machine of the government is there for all to see, but the internal workings are hidden from view. Externally, we see the buildings with the granite columns, the golden plaques, the waving flags and the politicians with the perfectly groomed hair and smiles. Inside, the mechanism is that of double-dealing psychopaths who spend their time jostling for political positions that accumulate power over your biology.

You will seldom, if ever, hear a meaningful truism concerning the nature of man from the mouth of a politician. They do not speak in these terms. The larger truth is their nemesis. They must continually skirt around the issues to avoid any penetrating question that a larger truth might spawn.

Ask yourself what kind of human would want to be a politician. It is totally possible that some politicians are well meaning. However, it is hardly possible that any successful politician is a truth teller. It is for this reason that you ought to forgo any worship or even the slightest partiality to any politician. They have a hidden agenda, even if they themselves are blind to it. Psychopaths rarely engage in self-reflection and have little, if any remorse.

Addendum

The following is selected from the book, *Stored Labor, a New Theory of Money* by Hugh A. Thomas © 1991

On inflation

Money in the form of coin originated with the Lydians in about 700 B.C. These coins were of private mintage and originated with the merchants and goldsmiths.

As metals evolved into usage as money, governments took control of these metals by the imposition of monopolistic practice. All coin was the carry the inscription of a god or the dictator's likeness. To the masses, this powerful symbolism was psychologically overwhelming. It was an ominous reminder to those under state control that the image of all the All-Powerful was stamped upon their labor and productive lives. Coinage was mostly limited to the government mint. Thus, the stage was set for inflation. As coin passed through the hands of the government, the coin was often re-alloyed with lesser quality metals, shaved, clipped or drilled in order to expropriate small quantities with each cycle. As the Greek orator Demosthenes said in about 320 B.C.: "The majority of states are quite open in using silver coins diluted with copper and lead."

Citizens caught doing likewise were often put to death.

Coinage that was originally a private matter was slowly looked upon as being in the state's province, an exceptional entity that must be controlled and issued only by the government. The government's debasement of coin diluted stored biological energy. Coin clippings were made into new coins, coins that reflected the new lighter weight or less valuable metal. The unit supply of coins increased. A new cycle of clipping would resume, and more metal would disappear, finding its way into ever increasing numbers of lighter coins.

Coins that were formally robust in weight would in time be thin and light. Those in power would pocket the newly minted coin that was manufactured from the clippings. Their expenditure in the marketplace would increase the number of monetary units in the economy without increasing a corresponding amount of goods. Prices were driven higher. Those coins that were once gold would often be reissued by government in a new and less valuable metal. This is a pattern of government lust for the expropriation of human productivity that continues even today. Silver coin becomes a nickel/copper mix; copper coin becomes a cheaper zinc alloy.

Inflation is theft of labor by dilution. It is process of chicanery designed by its perpetrators as a method of bypassing the more overt methods of labor expropriation such as taxation or physical enslavement. One should understand that the taxation/enslavement/inflation/property-seizure axis had one common denominator and one goal only: State seizure of labor, which translates to *state seizure of biological energy*. One should also understand that this process is thousands of years old and has been the basic modus operandi of every government.

Government entry into the game of the issuance of paper receipts for governmentally stored gold and silver is a historic study of fraud on the grandest scale ever devised in the history of mankind. This fraud was very slow in development and required a pre-existing condition of the psychological severance of money to self, of money to labor. After centuries of government meddling in coinage and debasement, the stage was set for the introduction of the least understood and greatest scam in the annals of history: paper currency issued by government.

On fiat paper currency

Man has the ability to pass from generation to generation scientific progress and ever-increasing knowledge of production techniques. In the same fashion, the knowledge possessed by thieves moves parallel to this progress. No doubt, while the methods of row-crop agriculture were first being invented by one man, another was waiting in the wings to steal his production as soon as the darkness of night was available. While the scientists of the enlightenment were breaking new ground in the understanding of physical nature, thieves were busy with the creation of central banks and paper notes.

These notes were originally receipts, i.e., substitutes for actual money. This fact of history is of premier importance. Gold or silver was deposited into a private bank or with a goldsmith for safe-keeping. A receipt was issued. These receipts were similar to a pawnshop ticket: the deposited gold or silver was redeemable to the person holding the receipt. As time went by, people quite naturally found that the receipts could be traded for goods; since the receipts were in fact title to the deposited gold or silver, they carried value at par in the marketplace.

If Mr. Jones wished to trade ten ounces of gold to Mr. Smith for Smith's champion hunting dog, Smith would quite likely accept a deposit receipt for ten ounces of gold in place of the actual metal, provided, of course, that the bank or goldsmith where the receipt originated was of sound reputation. It should be noted here that this receipt is a money substitute; the receipt itself has no stored labor value (other than the very small amount of labor extended to make the paper).

It should also be noted that in this transaction, strictly speaking, Jones not only purchased the dog, but Smith also purchased the gold. Exchange is a two-way street. These two commodities displayed the attributes of labor. The dog was a product of human labor, the labor of the domestication, breeding, feeding, grooming, etc. The gold was mined and refined. Gold that exists a mile under the ground in an undiscovered location has no value to Smith. A wild dog running across the plains of Africa will not retrieve duck for Jones. The attributes of labor gave these commodities their value. The men traded labor. Smith traded his labor of domestication, breeding, and training for Jones's labor that was represented as mining, smelting, etc.

That Jones may not have mined and refined his own gold is of no consequence. He possessed the labor that was expended to fabricate the gold. That the gold carried with it the attributes of human labor, that these attributes were passed along from the miner to his workers, to the baker, to the farmers and eventually Jones, makes no difference. The possession of these attributes, as expressed in the concept ownership, is the primary principle involved. The stored labor that was represented by the gold was Jones' labor, in that he owned it. Their medium of exchange was the atmosphere of non-violence.

In the same fashion that they were fascinated by coins, and for reasons of achieving the same ends, governments were fascinated by these money substitutes. These pieces of paper held the secret of the alchemist's dreams: obtaining gold (labor) from a common material.

Project your imagination into the past and visualize an economy functioning on this level. Now let your imagination place your mind set as one of a thief or crook. You see people trading pieces of paper with a par value to gold. You see an ever increasing public confidence in these receipts. Now what do you do? If you were a thief of average intelligence, you would probably print a few bogus receipts yourself. However, if you or your gang possessed governmental power, you would devise a way to take control of these receipts, first on a psychological level with symbolism, as those before you did with coin, and then slowly move in a step-by-step fashion into total control of the issuance of these receipts.

This is exactly what governments have done, and the horrors that man has experienced since governments have ventured into the arena of the issuance of paper notes have filled many volumes. The historical record is plump with descriptions of fiat note inflations.

One of the many problems in the nature of fiat notes (government currency) is that they afford no psychological anchor to objective measurement of entities in the real world. Their nature is that of an abstraction out of context to any sensory evidence of value. Regardless of a person's mental capacity for abstraction, man's knowledge of his life, work and savings is best felt when connected to the concrete. The loss of long-term savings and capital investment due to this psychological factor alone is beyond calculation.

Governments have attempted to shore up this deficiency by the use of symbolism. However, symbolism is not a replacement for the real thing, and history has proven this fact time and again. People prefer precious metals to scrollwork when psychological uneasiness becomes apparent to them, and they flee from paper. The question is one of degree: How much damage has been done to savings and capital investment by the non-apparent, i.e., the subconscious uneasiness that is ever-present in a fiat currency system?

Very few people have a conceptually defined definition of money, but the overwhelming majority of people must at least have a vague feeling that their money is the representation of their work, their productive life. If people feel uneasy about the soundness of the vehicle for their stored labor, their biological energy, they will quite naturally move their labor out of the paper currency in question and into other goods. This "flight to real values" is in a crawl today. That people have abandoned a high savings rate in favor of millions of electronic widgets, baseball cards, overpriced real estate and high debt, is quite possibly a symptom of this small but nagging psychological uneasiness.

One should understand that it has only been twenty years since the US dollar has been severed from gold on an international level. Since 1971, the entire world has abandoned receipts for gold and turned totally to the receipts themselves. The question is not one of *if*, but rather *when* the system will fail.

The factors that will bring on the failure are basically the growth of the state and the inevitable crisis of confidence that the impending labor dilution by paper money printing will bring about. When one considers the short history of fiat notes in relation to the length of time that commodity monies were in use by man, one wonders how long the system will hold together with the weak binding that is the symbolism of the state and the psychological glue of ignorance.

On paper money (fiat notes) and inflation

As we have seen, commodities have the attributes of labor. Man can therefore store his labor via these attributes. An obvious example is the man with the basket of nuts. If he collected more than needed for his immediate consumption, his accumulated labor would be over and above his current needs at the moment. If X amount of nuts were necessary to exist for one day, but he instead collected 10X, he would be then able to exist for ten days without expending labor to collect food because he accumulated or stored his labor for future use.

If these nuts were commonly traded or exchanged in a primitive economy, they would then function as money as they have the attributes of stored labor and are exchanged generically. As the economy grew, a new money would surface to replace the nuts, which are subject to insects, rotting and variations in quality. The people might then turn to salt, then skins, then finally to gold. All through this process, these monies are usable commodities that have the attributes of labor. They are valuable because they have utility, utility created by labor. When men trade these commodities they are therefore literally exchanging their labor.

Governments enter the picture. They are after labor. They first take slaves, which is highly inefficient. Productivity is low in a slave society. Slaves also revolt. Governments then learn to shave coin. People accept this shaving because they are mystified and intimidated by the symbolism. Their delusional mindset is carefully propagated and maintained by government propaganda.

Governments then print receipts for this coin; then they outlaw the coin. (In 1933, President Franklin D. Roosevelt signed executive order number 6201, which made it a crime to own gold. Citizens were required to turn over their gold certificates, gold coins and gold bullion to the government in exchange for paper currency that had no redemption value. With this one order, Roosevelt managed to seize the stored biological energy of millions of Americans.)

Finally, the government is totally in control of money. People are duped. They believe in the symbols on the paper. They have faith in the engravings: the past presidents, eagles, pyramids, queens, dictators, references to God, the fancy scrollwork, all of which are placed on the paper to mystify the people and give them a feeling of awe and fear.

You use this paper. It represents your labor. You have faith in it. You have used it most of your life. Let us assume that you have a total savings of one hundred thousand dollars. You plan to retire next year, after working and saving for nearly fifty years, and buy a retirement home in the woods. You wake up one morning and get ready for work. As you attempt to open your door to leave your home, the door does not open. Something is blocking it. You strain to open it by pushing whatever is blocking it out of the way.

When you look outside you see paper money, paper money by the trainload. It is at least a foot deep. Your first thoughts are to collect it, so you quickly reach down and start picking it up as fast as you can. You then stop after a few minutes and wonder what is going on. Hell, you couldn't pick it all up in a year. You are rich!!! You look down the street, and this paper money goes as far as you can see, on everyone's lawns, houses, automobiles — everywhere. People are busy with boxes, trash-cans and anything they can get their hands on collecting money. Your neighbor is loading his pick-up truck with money. You decide something is wrong: it is either a wonderful dream or a nightmare. You quickly drive to the market to pick up a newspaper to see what is going on.

When you get to the market, the man running it says that the newspaper will be fifty billion dollars. You are at first startled, but there is at least a billion times that much on the streets! Later the reality hits you, you think of your life savings, your stored labor. You have worked all your life to save your one hundred thousand dollars, and a newspaper now costs fifty billion. You are "rich," but you and your life savings have been wiped out. The productive part of your life that you have saved and stored is gone. This is the principle of labor dilution.

The principle is: Any time there is an increase in the supply of fiat notes, the stored labor that they represent is diluted. Since fiat notes have no corresponding attributes of labor to the value that they represent, they are disconnected from physical reality and are therefore easily manipulated by governments.

Afterword

Many people fear a small government, not because they are worried about the plight of the poor, but rather, because they worry that when they are no longer allowed to function as a parasite their world will fall apart. It is difficult to convince a vampire that blood sucking is depraved. However, little of this fear is warranted. Far more danger lies in oppressive government than with poverty in a free market. With a highly limited government, the great majority of people live better lives. With minimal taxation, charities flourish.

Over the years I have been asked many questions by my friends and skeptics. Some of the questions are:

"What about poor people? Who will take care of them?"

"What about the old and crippled? How will they make it without help?"

"What about education? Without public schools, children will not learn how to read or write."

"What about the administration of the airwaves?"

"Won't everyone have drug addictions without government control of drugs?"

To get things out in the open: It is not my responsibility to outline a course of action that solves all of these problems. In fact, it is not my responsibility to shape a course of action that solves *any* of these problems, not a single one.

What is offered here are facts about your biology and how these facts point to your biological requirement to live free from intraspecies parasitism, and how the psychopathic misanthropists have used lies, delusion and murder to block these facts from your mind.

If you are a metallurgist and discover that some alloys under stress will expand in ways that cause their premature deterioration, and then people object because you haven't outlined a cure for the camshaft in their lawnmower, the nails in their roof, or the wheels on their bicycle, *that is their problem*. You have given the world new ideas, and *that is enough*. Reasonable people can now take these ideas, do some mental work themselves, and project these ideas towards specific circumstances.

It is a burden to explain things to people who just cannot understand the difference between principles and specifics, but now I have the solution: I can refer them to this page.

For an excellent refutation of many of the statist's economic arguments and the answers to the above economic questions, see the book *Capitalism: A Treatise on Economics* by George Reisman in the recommended reading list.

Notes

1. The Chimpanzee Sequencing and Analysis Consortium. 2005. Initial sequence of the chimpanzee genome and comparison with the human genome. *Nature*. 437 (7055): 69–87. "We calculate the genome-wide nucleotide divergence between human and chimpanzee to be 1.23%, confirming recent results from more limited studies."

2. Sandy Woo, M.S. National Genome Research Institute. http://www.genome.gov/DNADay/q.cfm?aid=785&year=2010

"The basic structure of DNA (i.e., double helix) is shared among all living organisms. The code or sequence of DNA (instructions for our cells) is different. Even so, our DNA is likely more similar to plants than different. For example, we share approximately 60% of our DNA with a banana plant."

3. University of Alberta.

http://www.ualberta.ca/~chrisw/howfast.html

"The best answer for this question can be obtained because we have good estimates for the three main variables that enter into it: how many neurons (brain cells) we have, how fast a neuron can fire, and how many cells it connects to. A human being has about 100 billion brain cells. Although different neurons fire at different speeds, as a rough estimate it is reasonable to estimate that a neuron can fire about once every 5 milliseconds, or about 200 times a second. The number of cells each neuron is connected to also varies, but as a rough estimate it is reasonable to say that each neuron connects to 1000 other neurons- so every time a neuron fires, about 1000 other neurons get information about that firing. If we multiply all this out we get 100 billion neurons X 200 firings per second X 1000 connections per firing = 20 million billion calculations per second."

4. Meghan Neil. *For One Second a Supercomputer Mimicked the Human Brain.* http://motherboard.vice.com/blog/for-one-second-a-supercomputer-mimicked-the-human-brain

5. Ben Carson, on Charlie Rose. PBS, 2007.

6. CNN Labs. http://www.cnn.com/2012/10/12/tech/human-brain-computer/index.html

In context to the *Human Brain Project,* Sean Hill is commenting on the complexity of the human brain: "The computing power needed to build the model is phenomenal. Simply to replicate one of the 10,000 neuron brain cells involved in the rat experiment took the processing capacity usually found in a single laptop. To simulate a fully functioning human brain, it would take billions."

7. Gillian Gillison. "Fertility Rites and Sorcery in a New Guinea Village." *National Geographic Society.* July 1977: 124-146.

"To catch a killer, elders gather in a secret clearing with wild possums. The Gimis believe a dead man's sprit takes refuge among the marsupials, waiting to name his enemy.

"A sweet potato is offered to a caged possum as a name is whispered. If the animal takes a bite, potential guilt is indicated. Next the possums are killed and live caterpillars, representing suspects are wrapped in leaves, attached to their limbs and cooked. Then the dead man's relatives examine each insect for any signs of life – proof of guilt."

8. In 1980, I undertook an unpublished study to list edible plants. The major ones we all know such as rice, wheat, corn, potatoes, soybeans, etc. Then there are vegetables such as, lettuce, beets, several types of beans, tomatoes, turnips, carrots, broccoli, peppers, peas, celery, onion, etc. The lesser known and little used ones such as bok choy, jicama, celeriac, mints and many more were also listed. My total list was less than 300. If we add another 2,700 items to this list to account for local foods worldwide we get a total of 3,000, which is only 1% of the more than 300,000 plant species known.

9. Hugh A. Thomas. *Stored Labor: A New Theory of Money,* 1991.

9a. Jung Chang and Jon Halliday. *Mao: The Unknown Story.* New York, NY: Anchor Books, 2005.

9b. Dart Center for Journalism & Trauma a project of Columbia Journalism School
http://dartcenter.org/content/camp-z30-d-survivors#.UxggP179rjg

10. For a list of mass murders by government, see Dr. R.J. Rummel's excellent website: http://www.hawaii.edu/powerkills/welcome.html

11. http://www.davemanuel.com/history-of-bank-failures-in-the-united-states.php
A History of Bank Failures in the United States.
"The highest number of bank failures in one year since 1900 was 4,000. This took place in 1933."
Also see the FDIC list: http://www.fdic.gov/bank/individual/failed/banklist.html.

12. Henrik Svensmark and Nigel Calder. *The Chilling Stars: A New Theory of Climate Change.* London, UK: Icon Books Ltd, 2007.

13. http://georgereismansblog.blogspot.com/search?updated-min=2010-01-01T00:00:00-08:00&updated-max=2011-01-01T00:00:00-08:00&max-results=6

14. http://www.epa.gov/agriculture/ag101/demographics.html

15. Forest Preserve District of Cook County, Illinois. "Earthworms." Nature Bulletin No. 359-A: November 22, 1969.
http://www.newton.dep.anl.gov/natbltn/300-399/nb359.htm
Penn State survey shows 39,000 to 5,000,000 earthworms per acre in various soils and conditions.
See:
http://extension.psu.edu/plants/crops/soil-management/soil-quality/earthworms

16. http://earth.usc.edu/classes/geol150/stott/glbwarming/Termite%20Methane.htm
"Each termite produces, on average, about half a microgram of methane per day, a seemingly insignificant amount. However, when this is multiplied up by the world population of termites, global methane emission from this source is estimated to be about 20 million tonnes each year."

17. http://www.npr.org/blogs/thetwo-way/2011/11/03/141946751/along-with-humans-who-else-is-in-the-7-billion-club

18. http://www.petitionproject.org/

19. George Mason University News Network. *The Horrifying American Roots of Nazi Eugenics.* http://hnn.us/article/1796
Also see: Edwin Black. *War Against the Weak: Eugenics and America's Campaign to Create a Master Race, Expanded Edition.* Westport, CT: Dialog Press, 2012.

20. http://en.wikipedia.org/wiki/Eugenics

21. http://www.theguardian.com/lifeandstyle/2009/jun/21/quotes-by-prince-philip

Recommended Reading

History of dictatorships and their murders
Jung Chang and John Halliday. *Mao: The Unknown Story*. New York, NY: Random House, June 2005.
Robert Conquest. *The Great Terror: A Reassessment*. New York, NY: Oxford University Press, May 1990.
Stéphane Courtois, Nicolas Werth, Jean-Louis Panné, Andrzej Paczkowski, Karel Barto. *The Black Book of Communism*. Cambridge, MA: Harvard University Press, Oct. 1999.
R.J. Rummel. *Death by Government*. New Brunswick, NJ: Transaction Publishers, 1994.
Earth Science
Ian Pilmer. *Heaven and Earth*. Boulder, CO: Taylor Trade Publishing, 2009.
Fiction
George Orwell. *1984*. New York, NY: Penguin Group (USA), 1950.
Economics
G. Edward Griffin. *The Creature from Jekyll Island: A Second Look at the Federal Reserve*. New York, NY: American Media Publication, 2010.
Henry Hazlitt. *Economics in One Lesson*. Introduction by Walter Block. Auburn: Ludwig von Mises Institute. 2008. PDF version: http://mises.org/books/economics_in_one_lesson_hazlitt.pdf
George Reisman. *Capitalism: A Treatise on Economics*. Ottawa, IL: Jameson Books, 1996.
George Reisman. *The Government Against the Economy*. PDF version: http://mises.org/books/governmentagainsteconomy.pdf

Psychopathy

Robert Hare. *Without Conscience: The Disturbing World of the Psychopaths Among Us.* New York, NY: Guilford Publications, Inc., 1999.

Envy

Helmut Schoeck. *Envy.* Translated by M. Glenny & B. Ross. New York: Harcourt, Brace and World Inc., 1966.

www.ingramcontent.com/pod-product-compliance
Lightning Source LLC
Chambersburg PA
CBHW060938040426
42445CB00011B/912